JOURNEY INTO EDEN

WWI ADVENTURES IN THE MESOPOTAMIAN MOTOR MACHINE GUN CORPS

WAR HISTORY JOURNALS

Out of respect to a good soldier, serving in a difficult theater.

.

CONTENTS

INTRODUCTION

In 1914 Iraq didn't exist. Mesopotamia was a geographical expression that meant, "The Land between Two Rivers." It referred to modern day southern Iraq between the Euphrates and Tigris rivers. The Iraq we know today was created from three provinces of the Turkish (Ottoman) Empire—Mosul, Basra, and Baghdad.

By the start of the Great War, Mesopotamia was a political, military, and economic backwater in the Ottoman empire. It contained the two Shia holy cities of Karbala and Najaf. As well as linking to India and Iran (Persia). Mesopotamia was known as the Garden of Eden, Cradle of Civilization and the birthplace of Abraham in Ur. The city of Basra was an important port as well as being the home port of Sinbad the Sailor.

The British had maintained a strong diplomatic relationship with the Ottoman empire since 1815. Britain even joined the Ottomans against the Russians in the Crimean war. The Ottoman Empire was a useful ally against expansion into India and Central Asia.

British merchants traded in the Arabian Gulf since the

17th century. The British had negotiated and signed diplomatic treaties with the Gulf sheiks. By the 19th century the British/Indian merchants dominated trade in the Gulf. The Royal Navy supported them with anti-gunrunning, anti-slavery, and anti-piracy operations in the Gulf.

While the British dominated shipping between Baghdad and Basra, others moved in to irrigate the desert in hopes of returning the region to its fertile past. Everything changed in 1908, when oil was discovered in Iran. Known today as BP (British Petroleum). They created an oil refinery at Abadan Island in the Shatt-al-Arab waterway between Mesopotamia and Iran.

In the 1890s, Germany challenged British dominance in the region. German merchants traded in the Gulf and began to build the Baghdad to Berlin railway. The German government looked to the Ottoman Empire for support in its aggressive policy of imperial expansion.

When the great war started the Allies tried their best to keep the Ottoman Empire neutral. Germany made the Turks an offer they couldn't resist—the return of territory lost in the Crimean war. The Turks signed a treaty with the Germans a day before Britain declared war on Germany. The clever Turks didn't join the war at first—they waited before picking a side.

Britain sent the 16th Indian Army to the Gulf. Their instructions were simple:

If the Turks remained neutral, protect the oil on Abadan Island.

If the Turks joined the Germans, protect the oil facilities by capturing Basra.

A week later the Turks attacked the Russian fleet in the Black Sea. The British-Indian 16th brigade captured the

Ottoman stronghold on the Al-Fao Peninsula in a stunning amphibious operation.

The British Army in Mesopotamia had over 400,000 men. The majority (over 70%) of who fought were from the Indian Army. The remaining troops were from Britain and her other allies.

This book isn't a history lesson of Allied actions in WWI Mesopotamia.

This is the story of Frank Wooten. He was an American who served as a British officer in a motorized light machine gun unit in the Middle East. His unit was equipped with Rolls Royce armored cars.

He relates his experiences in Mesopotamia as a junior officer with the British Army. He concludes with his account as an officer with the US Army on occupation duty in Germany at the end of World War I.

He took his risks as a soldier, even if assigned to lead the unit's transport/supply section out of concern for his safety. Mostly his view of desert warfare was that of a serving junior officer with no special access to decision making.

Wooten had superior language skills. He became so skilled in Arabic that his unit had additional assignments for him based on his ability to talk with the locals, including local officials.

The old British Army could be somewhat clubby, but it is clear that Wooten had contacts and prior introductions that got him into the tents and households of people where a less connected American would have had little access.

My goal was to incorporate a sense of World War I service in a theater rarely discussed. Many of the same cities and areas modern readers will know from recent actions in the Middle East. My hope is to give the reader a glimpse into

WWI Army life, and the give and take of battle without the grit and gore.

This is Frank Wooten telling his story in his words. Gathered and edited from a collection of letters, interviews, clippings, and his personal journal. Let's walk through the pages of history together from a storyteller's perspective.

Griffin Smith
War History Journals

BOUND FOR MESOPOTAMIA

My adventure started off the coast of Southern Italy in the city of Taranto. Reinforcements were being sent from England. The troops would arrive through the Cape of Good Hope in South Africa. From there, they'd trek the entire path north. Others took a train through France and Italy across the Mediterranean into Egypt. They'd take the Suez Canal, down the Red Sea to the Persian Gulf. The latter was shorter, but more brutal, given the rough terrain in the Mediterranean.

Taranto was accessible through a thin channel, less than 200 yards wide. The historic part of town was built on top of a hill. Winding stone-capped roads wrapped through the town. Gravel alleys served as streets. We walked through town, heard fisherman singing, whistling, and laughing. They enjoyed the day's mission ahead of them. We came to a stone archway with several women sitting around. They seemed to be generations of a family. One of the older women, the grandmother of the group, was blind. She sat knitting and sharing songs with her attentive family. The grandmother sang without pausing to breathe. I carried on and was pushed back to reality.

The "rest-camps" in Taranto, best described as neat rows of tents on top of dying grass, is where we waited for our orders. No one knew what the Navy Commander had chosen for our fate. This campsite seemed more dismal than others. The Commander was Admiral Mark Kerr. He led the Mediterranean troop. He decided who would join his crew on the HMS *Queen*, one of seven ships of the Royal Navy. I was chosen to be his guest, a marvelous opportunity.

In the British Empire, the Navy was the highest-ranked service in the nation. It was easy to understand why the officers responded and acted the way they did. They were well-traveled and well-read. They shared stories of their adventures about the distinguished writers and statesmen they'd encountered along the way. We waited for the weather to break to make the journey as smooth as possible.

The admiral wrote poems along his journey. One that stood out was "Prayer for the Empire," which the German Emperor respected. He ordered it distributed to the German Naval recruits. The Kaiser's feelings toward the admiral did eventually change. Luckily, the German Emperor heeded the original warning:

> "*There's no menace in preparedness, no threat in being strong; if the people's brain be healthy and they think no thought of wrong.*"

* * *

AFTER FIVE DAYS passed on the HMS *Queen*, we transferred to the Union-Castle Line. A straight run to Busra, in Southern Syria. From there we boarded a sub and steamed out of the harbor. Two small Japanese Destroyers were there to protect us. We felt the rigidness of the submarine in the Adriatic. We only traveled at night for the first part of the voyage. It was difficult to explain how they maneuvered the submarine through the night. We made the journey and avoided collisions.

The next afternoon was filled with preparation. We rehearsed how to abandon ship and located exits and lifeboats. We made emergency strategies for the unexpected. Some crew were put in charge of specific sections of the boat. They made sure everything was safe, and the liferafts were in working order. As the sun dropped, the night dawned, and everyone off-duty called in for the night.

Three sharp blasts woke everyone on board after midnight. The international danger signal. We knew our orders. Each of us grabbed a life jacket and made way to our deck-stations. Everyone organized in perfect order. The entire squad sought information and direction. The Ship's Officer announced he heard the boat take on water. He disappeared for twenty minutes. Everyone was uneasy about what came next. The next boat over, I listened to a Scotch Captain say with a twinge of excitement in his voice, "It looks as if we could go down. I've seen a rat run along the ropes of my boat!"

Moments passed. The Officer announced we weren't sinking. Our ship and one of the Japanese Destroyers had collided. The impact hit above the waterline. We later learned the Japanese ship, although hit, made it to port.

After the collision, our ship docked for a few days in a harbor on the Albanian Coast. We waited for a new Destroyer to escort us. We enjoyed the downtime. The next night we steamed on the HMS *Queen* to Navarino Bay, on the southwest edge of Greece. On board was Lt. Finch

Hatton's grandfather, one of the officers who commanded the Allied Forces in 1827. He helped remove the Turkish troops and establish Greek independence.

A few days passed, and the HMS *Queen* arrived at Port Said in North Egypt in the Suez Canal. We sailed through the Suez and pushed on into the Red Sea. In August, this region was hot and well known for its tropical conditions. We had no ventilation system, no lighting, we were in a box of steam on water. We were short-handed, and some of the group was sent below. If transferred, you'd never take clean air for granted again. It was almost as if we inhaled humidity.

Map of Mesopotamia showing region of the fighting

Many crew members suffered from heatstroke. The medical areas on the crowded ship were not full service or sanitized. After our first casualty, the military burial at sea was impressive. A row of men with rifles, heads bowed. After a short, standard burial reading, the body, wrapped in the Union Jack, slid over the stern of the ship. As it ended, we heard the ring of bugles, singing the tunes of "Last Post." The last note of that song was a cue for the rest of the shipmen to sing "Abide With Me."

The next morning, we steamed down the Red Sea into the Indian Ocean. We avoided contact with each other in case of another illness or virus that could spread among the crew. At that time, duties were light. We spent time reading, playing cards, and anything to pass the time—but also staying alert. The men playing the Bugles would break to play a game they called "House" from dusk until dawn. It was like a game of lottery, no skill required.

Each player had squares of paper with numbers written on them. One person drew from a bag of papers marked with numbers. He called them out, and those with the same number cover it until all numbers have been covered. First to finish wins and collects a penny from all other players. Another game was more popular but forbidden. Known as "crown and anchor," the advantage lies in favor of the banker. But he makes too rich of a profit, and it's considered unfair.

The HMS *Queen* sailed through the Strait of Ormuz. A strait between the Persian Gulf and the Gulf of Oman. For those who'd been through it, it was reminiscent of the days of European supremacy. When the Portuguese were lured to the Strait of Ormuz by a superior English force. The reinforcements never arrived. The Portuguese could only sail forth and attempt battle. The attempt was successful. But not before joining with the two nearest Admirals and their boats. The Portuguese commander sent the British a beautiful, crimson, ceremonial cloak. In return, the British sent back an engraved sword. They together made a pledge and threw their chalices into the sea. This goes to show what's changed in the last few centuries.

An inspection of the maps and letters proved the geographical makeup was accurate. This made the troops hopeful. The map creator was one of the greatest Portuguese poets at the time. He wrote most of his masterpiece, "The Lusiad," when exiled in India. For almost two decades prior, he led a fast life in the East. He described several harbors, curves of the shore, and smells of the sea, in his beautiful pieces.

Our next destination was Busra, Syria—about sixty miles from Shatt el Arab. A name given by the Tigris and Euphrates after their Kurna tour, another 60 miles to the north. As we entered the river there was a sandbar, it blocked traffic for large boats, like the ones in our convoy. This caused us to transfer to more accessible British Indian channels and vessels. We passed the Island of Abadan. Home of the Anglo-Persian Oil Company and its successful refineries. Vehicle transportation was valuable in this area. It kept the businesses afloat.

There was no country-living in the beginning. General Dickson, the Director of Local Resources, encouraged the upkeep of agriculture. He suggested local farming & gathering as staples of life. Still, transportation would be necessary. Railroads took up double tracks. You could ride these trains from Busra to Amara, or from Kut to Baghdad. But the stretch that combined the two had not been built. Not until after the troops had left the country.

Along the roads, we saw over five-thousand Fords. On many of these trips, they took small groups of infantry to and from the base and destination. The cars would fit six: five men, plus the driver. At this point, everyone was turned into a driver. We'd seen trolleys in France with Indian and Indo-Chinese drivers. It was something new but didn't seem to faze many residents.

Busra stood on the banks of Ashar Creek. The ancient city where Sinbad the Sailor began his journey to the inlands. Buried deep under the shifting sands of the desert floor. Busra was a port for the last few centuries. Before that, Kurna was the chief seaport, and the two nearest rivers joined in the nearby ocean. They'd enlarged the continent and pushed back the sea. The continent changed at 12 feet per year. It didn't seem to be slowing down any time soon.

The town developed with the arrival of the Expeditionary Force. Most of the improvements needed were to fix the roads and valleys. It resulted into a permanent structure to go with the changes in the settling of the land. The British made striking improvements to the Mesopotamian region. If you want to conquer a country, you must develop it. The British built railways, roads, bridges, and power line systems. We wouldn't want to take over a country when it's run-down.

Ashar Creek at Busra

After landing in Busra, we had time to mingle and look around. We tried to gain our bearings. Bazaars were scattered across the land, also called "Suq" by the Arabs. The best bazaars were in Busra. It wasn't pawn items or art treasures that attracted people—it was the way the salesmen approached. The way they'd sway you, how they grouped items together to encourage a bigger sale. Every type of person could be found in the narrow aisles of the bazaar. Arabs, Armenians, Indians, Kurds, Chaldeans, you name it. They gathered and lingered at these hot spots. Near the entrances were booths of lamps and lanterns. *Aladdin-Ibn-Said* written above them, a reference to end slavery.

A few days after arriving in Busra, we were given a paddle-wheel boat. We used it to make our way up-stream —five-hundred miles into Baghdad. Along the river banks stretched miles and miles of palm trees. The Arabs worked on the plants, fertilized them, and trimmed them. These trees depended on human contact to transfer pollen. At Kurna, a Village in Egypt renamed *Al Qarnah*, we entered the Garden of Eden. I'll always remember this majestic sight and the feeling that I was walking through the pages of history. One of our crew members, Tommy, said "If this is the Garden, it won't take no bloody angel with a flaming sword to take me back."

It seemed not everyone shared my respect and wonder. Palm fronds fell from the trees. They were heard and seen everywhere. We watched as the natives feasted on the fruits.

North of Kurna, the river was no longer lined with palm trees. It changed into a swampy smell, a desert-like feel, home to lizards, and Arab marsh alligators. The gator would show himself, then slither back to water and safety once troop members got too close. On the banks of the Tigris lay Ezra's Tomb. It was in good condition. A sacred and holy place to Muslins, Jews, and Christians alike.

The next night, our paddleboat landed in Amara, Nubia. Nightfall was calm, and the wind had a slight chill. It was a relief for the desert-like conditions of the previous days. When we landed, we were free to scope out the land ashore. Down the bank and over the bridge, soldiers stood watch. They were clean, efficient, and on high alert. If anyone approached, we heard the echo of a booming, "Halt, who goes there?"

Outside of armored boats and monitors, river traffic was controlled by the Inland Water Transport Service (IWTS). The officers put in command there were pulled from all over. Most felt that nothing else mattered except what the officer of the IWTS would confirm while navigating. A light load, but enough to fulfill requirements. Everything from penny-steamers to the Thames River Craft would take that path.

On the HMS *Queen*, it was customary to have barges attached to either side. The barges were filled with troops, horses, and supplies. Next would be the first Bengal regiment. A new experiment by the current political parties. The Bengali were the Indians who quickly adapted to European ways. Rabindranath Tagore would be the most famous to do so. They went to Calcutta University and learned basic English language. They also learned general knowledge about the background of their destinations. This helped the Bengalis form the Babu class—many employed by the train system. They worked through the toughest vocabulary words. Afterward, they were ready to learn, grow and adapt. As a race, they were taught to be vain but positive. They prepared to deal with any grievances against the British government. The British felt it would put them at ease to be recruited and sent to Mesopotamia. They started with drills and were eventually used for attacking Baghdad.

Upon leaving Amara, we continued upstream. There was a boat a few hours ahead, but still only a couple hundred yards through the desert. The banks were extremely flat terrain. It made it appear other vessels were on actual land. The Arab river craft was flattering to the eye —at sunset, making headway with a full sail. The Arab women walked along the shore alongside the boat. They gathered baskets of eggs, chicken, and whatever the market had that day. From the boat, sailors tried to buy items, and it usually turned into a back-and-forth bartering.

One night, the ship stopped where not long ago, the last

of the Sunnaiyat Battles had been fought. For months, the British were held back. Their troops in Kut heard the shots fired and hoped that those sounds would not get any closer. The first part of the campaign was treacherous. Like the trench warfare in France.

The week before was a failed attempt at an attack, right before the surrender of the garrison. A year later, the position would be assumed by another. This area had a gloomy presence, even for a battlefield. Tons of shell casings, unexploded grenades, and bones scattered the field.

In Kut, it would be another 100 miles to get to Baghdad by train. It was better than taking the longer route through the curvy rivers and rough canals. A higher chance of being caught by shifting sandbars. At first look, Kut could be mistaken for unpromising land. Blazing heat and sand-and-mud houses. Despite the appearance, it was a thriving town.

The railroads ran through the desert, following the old caravan route to Baghdad. Half-way through we passed through Ctesiphon, almost 150 feet long and 80 feet wide. The arch stood 85 feet high and was surrounded by the ancient city now covered in sand mounds. Incomparable to the more ancient Mesopotamia, founded by Alexander the Great.

On our first night in Baghdad, General Maude invited some of the sailors to his house on the river. He was a military-type man, well over six feet tall. His military career was impressive. He started out in the Coldstream Guards, making his identity in South Africa. Early in the current war, he was injured in France. While in recovery, he took over the Thirteenth Division. He commanded the Gallipoli campaign, which was later brought over to Mesopotamia. When he reached the East, the situation was unpleasant. General Townsend was surrounded in Kut, and the Turks came out successfully. At the end of August, in 1916, four months after the fall of Kut, Gen. Maude took over leadership of the Mesopotamian armed forces.

The following year, on March 11th, he occupied Baghdad to re-establish British prestige. One of the biggest miscalculations made by Germany concerned the Indian situation. They tried to cause enough chaos to overturn British rule while keeping the English distracted with other uprisings. This caused a desire to send troops to India rather than another country. The Emir of Afghanistan likely did more than any other citizen to overtake the German intrigue.

When Gen. Maude assumed command, the Holy War had yet to end. The Holy War was preached in the mosques. Jihad proposed to unite only the most faithful believers to fight the invading Christians. They wanted to give the war a more religious tone. The Germans hoped this would lead to mutiny throughout the Mohammedan troops. This would hinder British forces and add fuel to the fire of the Turks. By trying to win over as many Arabs to their side as possible. The Turks oppressed the Arabs, as well as the Orientals, due to their brutal treatment. Under British rule, the playing field was more leveled-out. When a race had been neglected for so long, it would suddenly find itself to be equal with its enemies. This caused a negative feeling on all sides.

Most of the sailors read *Arabian nights* in their younger years. They remembered the lure of the luxury and romance in the East. The glamor in that book would be far from reality. In the bright Mesopotamian sun, it looked rough and cheap. Many years were spent searching the foreign land. Preparing systems and plans, for the depressing times ahead. It's unfortunate the standard expectations have changed. What would approach from the south would now come from all directions. The view of the city seemed flat. Outside, the palm trees lined the seashore yet again, and the Mosques towered above them. Further out were forests, flat roofs, and blue domes.

The covered bazaars consumed many hours of our day. I'd sit for hours at a coffee shop and people-watch through the windows. The lower-class Arab women, the veiled woman, and porters carrying their deliveries. Next door was a gold-and-silver market. Jews and Armenians hovered beside charcoal fires and haggled with customers and passerby. Many women carried their infants. It seemed impossible to me that the children—with such a low immune system—could survive in this place. They appeared to be well-fed and in good health.

Baghdad didn't become distinct until the 8th Century. As the home of the Abbasid caliphs, it was an influential position. Its greatness began toward the end of the 8th Century, under the rule of Haroun-el-Raschid. It went on to be a center of commerce and industry. Still, it suffered from sieges and conquests, as many of the surrounding areas. In the year 1258, the Mongols captured Baghdad under the command of Genghis Khan. They held it for over one-hundred years. Turned it over to the Turks, then Murad the Fourth. After all these changes and the site of many battles, it was not sought out by the caliphs.

There is little stone in Mesopotamia, also called "Cradle of the World." This was because of the traces of so many races and citizens that succeeded in ruling the land. When the Tigris height had gone down over the summer months, bricks would be dug out from its bank. Eighteen-inch squares that traced the seal of Nebuchadnezzar. All that remained before the arrival of the caliphs.

ARRIVAL IN BAGHDAD

A few days after arriving in Baghdad, the crew left for Samarra, which at the time was the Tigris front. Most troops were with the Royal Engineers. Led by Major Morin, an officer with an impressive resume from his time in France and Mesopotamia. The Third Indian Army Corps was the lead army in the Tigris, with General Cobbe in command. His troops were nicknamed the Victoria Cross.

Seventy miles of railroad separated Baghdad and Samarra. Built by the Germans, it was the Mesopotamian part of the well-known Berlin-To-Baghdad Railway. Well-constructed, with firm roadbeds, heavy rails, and steel beams made by Krupp. During their retreat, the Turks were in too much of a hurry to destroy more than burning down a few stations and blowing up water towers. The majority of what they left was intact.

No passenger coaches, we could only travel by flatcar or boxcar. We followed the Indian custom of carrying rolled-up mattresses, and a leather washbasin with washing kit. With a compact chair or stool. No travel water was provided, and we didn't know why. The trains were fitted with anti-aircraft guns. Turkish planes would drop bombs, it was harder to hit a moving target.

The trains left Baghdad in the dark hours of the night and early morning. The boat bridges were closed at night, forcing the troops to sleep on station platforms. Generals and staff officers had a car assigned to them. They would be brought up from the yard so they could turn in for the night. Often, the trip would be postponed. The sergeant-major would welcome their friends to enjoy a good nights' sleep. The train ride lasted 12 hours, but when using a bag of grains as a chair, the time didn't pass like we hoped. Crew members brought books, like the much handed-out *Vingt Ans Après*, to help pass time in the blistering heat.

Still far from Samarra, we caught the sun gleam on the golden tops of the mosque domes. They were built over the opening where the twelfth Imam was said to have disappeared. The myth was that one day he would re-appear to establish the true faith back on earth. Many Arabs claimed to be the twelfth Imam. This caused a lot of trouble, according to their followers. The most infamous would be a man that had surrounded Khartoum and captured the Asian General Gordon and his men. Now, twenty-five years later, we passed through the Sudan. There were few middle-aged men left, many had been wiped out under the fearful rule of the Mahdi. This possibly served as a prototype to the Germans in Belgium.

Golden Dome of Samarra

Rafting down from Tikrit

Samarra is ancient. It has lived through periods of great depression and equal-sized expansion. In 363 A.D., this was where the Roman Emperor Julian passed away from his injuries during the battle in Ctesiphon. The Golden Age lasted 40 years. In 836, Caliph Hutasim transferred capitals from there to Baghdad. The city extended twenty-one miles along the riverbank. Lined with gorgeous palaces and ruins, some still stood. The present-day village had shrunk from its original size. But still a beauty to look at with the solid walls and huge gateways. The residences closest to the walls were in shambles or sitting vacant.

In a more peaceful time, the Samarran climate drew in Baghdad families. They came to pass the summer months, using it as a retreat. Most residents were Persian, due to the eleventh and twelfth Shiah Imams buried on-site at the largest of the local mosques. The two major Islam followers are the Sunnis and Shiahs. The former shape of three Caliphs who followed the path of Mohammed as his successors. Many believed his son-in-law, Ali, along with their sons Husein and Hasan, were the prophet inheritors. Ali was assassinated near Nejef, a sacred city, and Husein was killed in Kerbela. These two cities were known as the greatest for Shiah shrines. The Turks belonged almost without exception to the Sunni sector. Persians and most Arabs living in Mesopotamia were the Shiahs.

Surrounding Samarra was a country similar in character to southern Arizona. The same barren hills existed, the same blazing heat. There is soil, not sand, ground to a fine dust permeating across every object. The dehydration here was considerable. We kept all our leather oiled. The covers of our books would crack and curl if not greased. In the lowlands, trench-digging was one of the more manageable tasks. Once we made it to the hills, the pebbles and rocks proved more difficult.

The tallies were even on both sides whether the Turk would try to advance down the Tigris. Things had gone badly with the Palestinian Forces during the first battle of Gaza. But, we had a terrible position, and the opinion was the enemy should think twice before an invasion. The base was located at Tikrit, thirty miles away. Another ten miles stood the small village of Daur. Where the Turks held a majority of their force. Between Daur and Samarra was a desert, and not much else. Gazelles and jackals were the only permanent inhabitants. In this no-mans-land, we had patrols on either side, who met occasional scuffles. For the reconnaissance work, we used the light-armored motorcars. Well known throughout the army as Lam cars, a name created by the first initials of everyone's title. The motorcars were Rolls-Royce, with armored-plate weight, adding between three and four tons. They were bulletproofed, but only to the ordinary bullet—not against anything armor-piercing. When I intended to make the trip to Mesopotamia, I planned to be transferred to the cavalry. But after seeing the cars at work, I changed my mind and asked to be assigned to the armored branch of service.

Word came in that the Turks had been congregating at Daur, and Gen. Cobbe had decided to push forth to meet them. We moved out one night and expected to give Abdul a surprise. We started too early and were spotted by the Turks airplanes, or we made too much noise—we never learned why. The enemy kept falling back, which caused some skirmishing and a few prisoners. But everything came to a halt. We weren't prepared to attack the Daur. We turned back to Samarra to wait.

I kept busy searching for an Arab servant. Seven or eight years prior, when my father was in Africa, I had picked up some Swahili. This helped in learning Arabic, but I'd forgotten a lot of what I'd learned. A majority of officers had British or Indian servants, known as "batmen" or "bearers." I decided to go another route and searched for an Arab who would help me learn the Arabic language.

Yusuf, a candidate of mine, was strong, and somewhat surly, for being only eighteen. Not 100% Arab, he claimed several backgrounds and took to them all, primarily being a Kurd. I felt there was a good percentage of Turk in him since his father was a non-commissioned officer in the Turk's army. I dreaded taking him along on patrols since he wouldn't be shown mercy if he fell into enemy hands. He insisted on coming, he didn't show much concern during the fighting. He spoke many languages with varying levels of fluency: Kurdish, Persian, and Turkish. All an excellent use for me. He was brought on and became a trusted and faithful servant. His only weakness was his high degree of devotion to me and was of little use to anyone else.

I had with me two horses: one named Soda, which meant "black" in Arabic, and the other I never named. He was a hard-headed horse. He had energy day and night, unaffected by the sounds of gunfire. He was stubborn about directions of where he would travel. I came up with a better way to deal with him—hire a Syce to look after him, a horse groomer. This Syce was a wild, unkempt character with a long, dark beard. He appeared knowledgeable yet was half-witted. Most of them are more or less insane, as goes the stereotype. A cause-and-effect from them being dervishes. Where natives are directed under the protection of God.

They go around practically naked, carrying large bowls. They also carried an iron bodkin, a pole with a wooden ball at the end, looking like a fool's knickknack. They led a simple life. They'd find a fancy house to settle down near the gate. The owner supported them as long as they needed to stay there until they got back on their feet. If they used force, they were looked at by the dervish as unfavorable. There was little doubt in my mind that they'd be capable of making any good use of the iron and steel rods. Why my dervish wanted to give this life up was beyond me, but he seemed to love the horses and had pure intentions. When he arrived dressed in an ancient gunnysack. I gave him a regulatory khaki outfit.

My duties took me on long rides throughout the country. Mesopotamia's amazing history continued to impress me. Everywhere I went there were ruins and large sand mounds. The desert crept in and claimed the land as its own. Dust-covered every palace, house, temple, and market, in its ever-lasting blanket of land. The weight of the ages was present as we rode among the ruins of these once habited, busy cities. Now long gone and buried, and for how long, no one knew. Names such as Babylon, Ur of the Chaldees, Nineveh, once popular now often forgotten—nothing but desert mounds.

Samarra stood like a colossal corkscrew tower, known by the natives as "Malwiyah." It was 160 feet tall and built of strong brick. A paved path wound up and around the outside. The purpose was unknown, it's age was claimed in a range as wide as several thousand years. Stories were told about the custom of executing prisoners by throwing them off the top of the tower. It was a magnificent observation post for us. A large mound rose from the desert floor about five miles up-stream toward the town.

The legend was when the Emperor of Rome died of his wounds, his soldiers built a mausoleum to impress the natives. It would have been impossible for a retreating army to have taken on something of that size. The locals called it "The Granary," claiming that would be the primary use. Before the war, the Germans excavated and discovered shafts that led through the foundation of the tops of the palace. Around the base were some barely-seen roadways and circular plots. Especially when the view was from over-head—it appeared to be an elaborate plot system for gardening.

We received false alarms and rumors about what the Turks' plan was. We believed they couldn't flank us with enough strength to be a serious threat. The only reports we got were few and far between. One afternoon our planes reported they'd viewed a concentration of Turks. Estimated at six to eight thousand, marching to our right flank. Our plane was instructed to verify the details. They returned at dark, with no update from their previous report. The night was dark and silent. High emotions ran through to the next morning. The vicious enemy was confirmed to be herds of enormous sheep.

We were ordered to carry out reconnaissance. How could we get a large force surrounded by water on a marsh? I left in an armored car with Capt. Marshall of the Intelligence Service. Capt. Marshall spent several years in Mesopotamia. He was well known and trusted by the Arabs along the Tigris from Kurna through to Mosul. The Captain spoke the language better than anyone in the troop. It tied to the accent of his Caledonian hometown in Scotland. With us were a couple of older Sheiks, and today was their first vehicle ride. One of them had a hard time covering his fear and maintaining his dignity. We weren't sure of the reason until we stopped, and he bolted out of the car, getting sick. It seemed ironic they ride 90 miles on a camel yet couldn't handle a car ride without motion sickness. It was challenging to get him back into the car. While searching for the Sheik, we discovered plenty of wells. More than what we thought existed, but not quite enough to use them as part of a flank attack.

The land tickled your eyes. Optical illusions made balloon observers cautious in their claims. In the early days of the campaign, the Battle of Shaiba Bund proved to be a friendly mirage. This saved the British forces from a wicked defeat. Suleiman Askari was commander of the Turkish forces. They discovered the Turks were in full retreat. Their leaders caught sight of the mirage. But it was just an ambulance and supply train. But so enlarged, they thought it was a large body of troops and reinforcements. When Mr. Askari was told of his mistake, he took his own life.

I advanced on the Turkish forces while at Daur. Gen. Brooking made a successful attack on the Euphrates. He captured the small town of Ramadi. It lay on the Euphrates river and held nearly five-thousand prisoners. The army commanders' intentions were to relieve the pressure put on by Gen. Allenby. His troops in Palestine attacked the enemy on all three fronts of the Mesopotamia. We marched at dusk, prepared to take the enemy down at daybreak. While the sun set, I caught a glimpse of Mohammedan soldiers pushing themselves through the Mecca during the evening prayers.

It was late October, and the days riddled with blinding sun rays, nights bitterly cold. A night-march had its pros and cons. The head of the columns would be checks and halts. The darkness meant the men in the back would have no idea if the troops' stops were voluntary or not. We shivered, longing for a cigarette, forbidden because it would give away our position in the dark. Throughout the night, we marched, halted, marched. The dust choked us. The hours blended together until 2 a.m. Word made its way through that it was alright to rest for an hour.

In Mesopotamia, the regulation army uniform consisted of a tunic and shorts. I use the term "shorts" loosely. They were long cut-off trousers that laid above the knee. We used leather leggings or stockings for insulation. A massive help in the heat since it left freer knee action and allowed the clothes to dry faster when wet.

We were drunk with sleep, it would've taken a lot to wake us up in one hour. But, at 3 a.m. we pushed on and attacked at dawn. The enemy abandoned the first-line positions, and we didn't have much resistance at first. Our cavalry concentrated through points in the river beds. They suffered at the hands of a hostile plane. The Turks decided to return to Tikrit, a city in Iraq, with a smaller defense. They could've given us a harder time than they did. Among the prisoners we took, only a handful of them were worthwhile. The Turkish officers were well-dressed and well-educated. Many of them spoke French. One of the best gunnery schools was in Constantinople. One of the captured officers had been a senior instructor there for many years.

Accompanying us was an intelligence officer Captain Bettelhein, born in Constantinople. He served with the Turks against Italy, as well as with the British vs. the Boers. This gunnery officer turned out to be an old comrade of Capt. Bettelhein during the Italian War. Most of the officers got to know him since he had been the Chief of Police in Constantinople. None of them gave him credit when they had found out they were serving against him.

The supplies we captured at Daur included many of our rifles and ammo the Arabs had stolen and sold to the Turks. It was impossible to prevent this. We guarded our dump as best we could. On the darker nights, Turks would creep into our camp. It wasn't safe to leave for the hospital to have our barges tied down to their riverbank. Many times, Arabs crawled aboard and killed off the injured. The Arabs played no favorites and attacked whichever side seemed more beneficial. During the fight at Sunnaiyat, the Turks sent someone to request a 3 days' truce. During that time, we joined forces against the Arabs.

The following night, we set up a temporary camp at Daur. We saw nothing other than a single enemy plane that came over to "lay eggs," so we pushed on to Tikrit. We made a light move, and if we found any Turk wanting to stay and fight, we were to stand down.

Gazelles had gotten into no-man's-land between the Turks and us. Even with rapid and constant gunfire, they would stop to watch in amazement and see the dust settle.

Later on, in a French forest, the same thing happened, but with wild boar. The enemy seemed less than inclined to evacuate Tikrit. We returned to the previous night's camp in Daur. On the walk back, we passed an old Turkish coupe, abandoned and alone in the desert.

The next morning's instructions were to march back to Samarra. Shortly before midnight, Gen. Maude changed our orders to advance on Tikrit. We halted and took stock of our newest orders. The cavalry yet again suffered at the hands of the Turk's airplane. I went to headquarters in the afternoon. A crowd of staff officers sat around a small table drinking tea and discussed the plan of attack for the next day. All of a sudden, a Turk plane flew low and dropped bombs at continuous intervals. It dropped two, then a third atop of a hill, making a straight line along the conclave. It seemed as if the next bomb would be a direct hit on us. The staff did the only thing they could do and took cover as flat on the ground as their bodies and nature would allow. The Hun's spacing was poor, and the next bomb dropped far off. I remember the excitement and laughter at what we thought was a joke.

Our anti-aircraft weapons were called "Archies," we mounted them on top of our trucks. They were hard to attach due to their heavy weight. I never forgot the joy when they finally got into view. I never got to see what was behind the Archies, but I had no doubt that they didn't bomb us with the same type of artillery.

That night, we marched on Tikrit. As dawn broke, we were ready to attack. The morning dew cleared. An alarming sight caught our attention. On the right, tractors hauled our heavier loads. They headed straight to Tikrit and made themselves into tanks. They discovered their mistake and turned around to make the best pace, about 3 mph.

Our weapons caused a good deal of damage. We trekked through a hilly, wide stretch of nothing but country to reach the Turks' front lines. At dark, the second line of the trenches was right in our hands. The cavalry circled around the flank that led up-stream to Tikrit. They would cut off the enemy if they attempted to retreat. The town lay on the right of the Tigris River. We had a small troop coming up from Samarra on the left river bank since there was no way to get crews across the river. We had over 2,000 casualties that day. The Seaforth's suffered the most, but not much more than the native regiments.

In Mesopotamia, there were many changes where the Indian battalions stood. The Mahrattas were not considered unusual, they had a lot of pride. The Gurkhas didn't live up to what they had expected. The Indian troops did well as a whole. There wasn't much reason to compare them with another. The Expeditionary Force and all of its branches, about a million, had come from India. We obtained our supplies in India and Australia. We preferred the canned beef from Australia over the American version.

At nightfall, the battle died down. We were instructed to hold and not go over until sunrise. I made my way back to headquarters. A General pounced on me and ordered me to get a car and travel as fast as possible to Daur. I was to bring back any motor ration-convoy with enough fodder for the horses as well as riders. A Ford car happened to pass me, the General stopped the car, opened the door, and shoved me in. He gave the driver instructions. Fifteen miles away, the country was chopped up by ravines and most areas had dead-end roads. They jammed up the two-lane roads in every direction.

We blew a tire about four miles from Daur. The driver had already used his spare. We had no choice but to try and make it by driving on the rim. The car was wagon-like, and while we stopped, I took stock of what I saw around me. I used what little vocabulary I had in his dialect. I realized it was too late to stop another car and send this guy back. We kept on going. Across one of the ravine beds and over a hill. I managed to grab a spare tire so we could get back. By that time, I took the wheel so we could make better time. My driver tried to explain he couldn't drive well at night either, adding fuel to the fire. When would we get back? What would I tell that General? If I could even find him again.

I took my illuminating compass and set out to steer this cross-country course. I ran into five groups of ambulances filled with the injured and dying, trying to also get back to Daur. Many were lost. Some gave up and stopped. Some headed back in the wrong direction, lost in the night. We had no vehicle headlights either, but I somehow knew the right way to go. All I could do to help the others was suggest the best direction, but I had to move on. I did end up finding headquarters. The General handed me some ham and a peg of whiskey—the first edible thing I had since morning.

That night, the Turks evacuated—their forces were mobile. They covered shocking distances living on the bare essentials. We followed in March and occupied their previous campsite. White flags flew from some of the houses, which weren't as damaged as we would imagine. It was surprising to see how much a town could take without a noticeable effect. It took a while to level a town the way they had done it in Northern France. In this region, the banks of the river averaged a hundred-fifty feet tall. Tikrit was built where they connected, the junction of the two ravines. No two streets seemed to be on the same level. Rooftops would be on a lower level compared to the houses on the next street up. Many bazaar booths were open, conducting business as usual.

Our men bought cigarettes, matches, and what vegetables were available. Yusuf had lived here before, so I sent him to get chickens and eggs for the mess hall. I ran into Marshall, on his way to eat with the Mayor, an old friend of his. He asked me to join, and I obliged. We climbed up a hill to a very comfortable house, built with a beautiful courtyard. It was the best meal we had eaten in what felt like ages —rice pilaf, bread, and chicken. The bread was thin, like a griddlecake. The Arab used it as a plate, since eating with your hands can be difficult, especially with rice. You're given a towel and soap after the meal is complete. One of the many formalities supposed to be acknowledged. Another being no one should eat or drink with their left hand.

In Tikrit, we didn't find as many supplies as we had hoped for. The Turk had destroyed most of the stores. We found large amounts of wood, which in this naked, tree-less country was worth a good penny. Most of the residents in Tikrit are raft commanders by profession. Their rafts were made in the same manner as the days of Xerxes and Darius. Inflated goat skins were used as pole platforms, cut in the forests up-stream. On these rafts, we started from Mosul, and goods would float down. When the products reached Tikrit, they left their poles behind. They headed up-stream on foot, carrying their deflated rafts. The Turks used this method in the pre-war days. They would come straight through Baghdad, but usually broke down by Tikrit. There was a long desert route that ran across the Euphrates. Supplies from up-stream would be taken across in camel caravans.

An aerodrome was six miles up the hill from the central

town. I was anxious to explore the comfortable houses the Germans built. I'd found a friend who's job required vehicle transit, and we set off in his car. A dust storm approached. We had trouble finding our way through the trenches. Once we got outside, a wicked storm raged, we could only see a few yards ahead. We were lost at one point and ran over the edge of a bluff. We gave up and worked our way back.

When we started on this trip, I was reading *Anabasis*. We were ordered to march into Tikrit by a captain of the Royal Flying Corps and ended up in the middle of the entire mess. I told him that I was close to being out of reading material. He loaned me another book, Plutarch's *Lives*.

After a few days, orders came to prepare to fall back on the trip to Samarra. The line of communication traveled through so many people. It was impossible to maintain good organization. Nine months later, when we had more train rails, a line was established to run to Tikrit. Abandoned by the Turks under threat of our attack on Kirkuk, in the Persian hills. It was tricky to explain to the troop members, particularly the Indians, the need for falling back. All they understood was that we took over the town at a high cost and were now about to give up.

I spent days helping to prepare the river rafts to take wood and other supplies worth coming with us. The river height was lower, so it left a long stretch of beach below the village. We removed the poles. Several camels died in or near the water, likely from shelling. The blinding heat made them unpleasant companions. The first day was terrible enough, but the second was even worse. The natives didn't seem affected. They brought their dirty laundry and worked among themselves. They came down near us to get their drinking water from the river, usually down-stream from the camels. The water percolated through the giant clay pots before drinking to purify it. On the third day, much to their surprise, we managed to tow the camels out.

We got the rafts built and stable, over 80 of them. We took on enough Arab pilots to take care of half of them. The rest were put on Indian sepoys. They made quite some hype when we got all the rafts moving down-stream. Two broke up in the rapids close to Daur, but the rest reached Samarra safely the following day.

We camped on the bluffs underneath Tikrit. High enough above the plain to be above the dust storms. The prospect of going back to Samarra was more pleasant to me than the other men. Five days after we took the town, we turned right around and marched in sync to the railhead.

ON PATROL IN BABYLON

We returned to find Samarra buried in dust, more desolate than ever. A rainstorm rolled in a few days later. After a night of pouring rain, the air was clear, and we were no longer enveloped in a cloud of fog.

It was a relief to see the heat-stricken camps all broken up. Over the summer months, our ranks thinned out in the blaring sun. The British suffered most, the Indians a close second. Before the camps organized correctly, the mortality rate was high. The only effective treatment required the use of ice, and we were in the desert. It was impossible to manage the ice machines and have them installed fast enough. The camps were situated in the coolest, most comfortable places, considering the conditions. Even still, death was a typical result, and the recoveries were only a small percentage. Men who had heat stroke were of little use in battle.

Another summer illness was Sand-Fly Fever. Caused by sand-fly bites, theses insects plagued the land. Sometimes it was so severe that the victim was sent to a military hospital in Baghdad.

The Tommies' felt passionately about not having the need to be "Cushy Blightly," in the Mesopotamian campaign. "Blightly" meant a wound that caused permanent disablement. Or caused the patient to be sent to India, or back to their home country, depending on the case. Due to this, there was a restriction on short leaves. There weren't many places we could go even if we wanted to.

At a rapid rate of travel, the illness took two weeks to get to India. Transit was difficult. Only under specific circumstances were you allowed to leave to England. One spring, it was announced to all officers who wished to get married or divorced that they could apply for leave with a decent rate of success. Several applied, but many men came back without having gotten married or divorced. The army commanders restricted all leave after that. They put all divorce files into the hands of another officer whose primary role was legal matters. He arranged for them to be processed without the need to go on leave.

A week after returning to Samarra, a rumor circulated that Gen. Maude was sick with cholera. A virus that caused severe stomach issues and dehydration. There were a few sporadic cases, but not enough to be considered an epidemic. One of the officers working with the military governor of Baghdad had died. We also heard the army commander had another form of this virus, and no one knew his chance of recovery. The death announcement was hard to take, the emotion of the whole site was blanketed with gloom.

The entire army had the utmost confidence in their leader and mourned his loss. The typical rumors of poison and foul play took its rounds. I learned from Colonel Wilcox that it was the same case as Baghdad's officer. Col. Wilcox was a renowned practitioner and had been with Gen.

Maude throughout the entire illness. The General never took any preventative measures for the disease. Regardless of how many times Wilcox urged him to.

Towing an armored car across a river

Reconnaissance

General Marshall took over, he'd commanded Gen. Maude's 13th Division. The seventeenth lost Gen. Gillman, who had since become chief of staff. This was a significant loss to their division. He was many of the troop members' idols.

My transfer to the Motor Machine-Gun Corps was approved. Assigning me to the Fourteenth battery of the light-armored cars, commanded by Capt. Nigel Somerset. His grandfather was Lord Raglan and died while in command of the British during the Crimean War. Somerset was in the infantry at the outbreak of the war, where he'd been wounded in France twice. A fantastic leader, with excellent judgment and an effortless magnetism. A battery was composed of eight armored cars, split up into 4 sections. They were Rolls-Royce cars, as well as some Napiers and Fords.

During that time, there were only four batteries in the entire country. We were an army of troops. We weren't assigned to any individual division or corps. We were temporarily assigned in scattered positions as the need arose.

In the attacks, we worked with the cavalry, there were occasions where they tried to use us as tanks. It was not a success since our armor-plate was too thin and lightweight. We were brought in to raid and quell Arab uprisings. This put us near political officers. An interesting group of men, some from the Army, most from civilian life. They took over civil administration of the newly-claimed territory. They proudly upheld native justice.

Some of these men had devoted a lifetime to the study of the inner workings of Oriental Diplomacy. They were distinguished by white tabs on the collars of their uniforms. Many political officers were executed in the isolated towns of the unsettled districts. We would often take a political officer along with us on raids or reconnaissance. We utilized their knowledge of the dialect and customs. Sir Percy Cox was the Chief Political Officer, and at the same level of rank as a General. His notable career in the Persian Gulf was due to the well-planned handling of delicate situations in Mesopotamia.

Miss Gertrude Bell assisted Sir Cox and the head of the Arab bureau. She had a direct relationship with the Expeditionary Forces. She spoke fluent Arabic and became interested in the East while visiting her uncle in Tehran. The capital of Iran, where he was a British minister. She made significant expeditions through Syria and Mesopotamia. She wrote many valuable books, including *Armurath to Armurath* and *The Desert and the Sown.* She held a position in high-regard and had to appear confident. Especially when the Mohammedan attitude towards women was that they were a subservient class. Miss Bell worked steadily, and without leave in the heat. Her judgment was solid and unwavering. Her actions contributed to British success.

The headquarters that oversaw the various batteries was located in Baghdad. There, we had a permanent array of stores and billets, temporary military facilities. We were often ordered into sections to distance ourselves, but rarely part of each battery for more than a couple of months. The officer of the workshop was in charge and had the task of keeping the cars maintained and in working order. The supply & demand of spare vehicle parts was tricky to manage. A high-level of skill was needed to be successful, Lt. Linnell of the Fourteenth was appointed.

A few days after joining, I set off with Somerset and another one of the battery officers, Lt. Smith of the Black Watch. We patrolled the ruins of Babylon. Kerbela and Nejef, the great Shiah shrines, were rarely friendly with the Turks, who were Sunnis. The desert tribes were also Sunnis. Their natural instinct to go raiding made them eager to take advantage during government suspensions. We organized an imitation police troop that was more for looks than effectiveness. They were armed with all sorts of weapons, varying in age by centuries, and from different origins. We referred to the wild desert folk as Budus. They were frequently armed with the rifles they'd stolen from us, making the odds far from even.

We set up shop in Museyib, a town on the banks of the

Euphrates seven miles above the Hindiyah Bridge. It was a dam that was finished a few years earlier. Originally designed to lure in a wealthier clientele to the country. We patrolled out on the desert's caravan route to Baghdad, down to Hilleh, into the ruins of Ancient Babylon. The rainy season had begun, our patrolling was irregular, opposite the rain. A twelve-hour rain made it impossible to have our heavy cars make it for two or three days straight. We had pleasant company with officers from the Punjabi infantry battalion, as well as Indian cavalry. We stole an ancient caravan-serai, specifically for billets. We used our downtime to clean it and make it as waterproof as we could with the circumstances and materials given. An oil drum was as long as an iron telegraph pole stuck in its top to provide a serviceable area to sit when it rained. We usually played bridge in it.

I was ready to take some weight off and make space for more books. Voltaire's *Charles XII* was the first book that carried me into their world at this moment in time. I always kept a volume of some sort on me. I'd find shade on the hood or trunk of my car and read during halts. Two volumes were my favorites, Layard's *Early Adventures* being one of them. The writer was a renowned Assyriologist. A student of history and agriculture, and the author of *Nineveh and Babylon*. The book I read was written in his early 20s but wouldn't be published until forty years later. Layard began life as a legal clerk in London but was offered a post in India where he thrived. Before Baghdad, he stopped in Kurdistan, Iraq. He became captivated by the tribesman's lifestyle. He chose to live with them for an adventure-filled two years.

I finished a translation of Xenophon and found it to be a different book from when I read it as a kid. I felt this because I took it in with a different view. Having a vivid scene of the battle of Cunaxa, Babylon, within sight of the Greeks, and through the loss of a leader. I appreciated what a masterpiece the retreat was. Xenophon referred to it as the "snow sickness," more simply put: starvation or freezing to death or a combination of both. Men died in the snowy banks of the Anatolian highlands. He wrote that if you built a fire and someone provided food, the sickness would go away.

The rain continued, it turned dirt into mud, everything sank deeper and deeper. It was all that the Arabs could do to get their produce to market. The bazaar wasn't big but still thrived. I used to sit in one of the coffee houses and drank coffee or tea while smoking a long water pipe called the narghile. At this point, my Arabic was fluent for ordinary conversation. I'd try to listen in on the gossip of the Arabs as I made my way through. Bazaar rumors were a way to get an intelligence advantage before reported by officials.

In Baghdad, I heard we launched an attack. When headed to headquarters, I mentioned the rumor I heard, no one there had yet heard about this but then, it happened. I had met with the natives in Africa and remembered how in the Civil War, the blacks were often the first to get the news of our battle. It was something I'd never heard explained well to anyone.

In the coffee houses, outside of smoking and gossiping, we played games like chess and backgammon. We also played Mancala, known as one of the most ancient games, dated as far back as the jackstones used in the game. The board was a log sliced in half and hinged together. We scooped the holes out to hold the stones and made it worthwhile.

In most places, the coffee was Arab fashion, not Turkish. The Turk's coffee is sweet and thick, and the tiny cup they give you was 50% coffee grounds. The Arab coffee was clear, buttery, and had a delicious flavor. The small porcelain cup was filled several times. Every time seemed like only one gulp of liquid was added to the muddled-up coffee grounds. The tea was served in even smaller glasses, without milk, but plenty of sugar. The small spoons provided with the glasses had straining holes to stir the tea without spilling it.

I never got tired of watching this one particular booth. The elderly man who owned this booth was a pickle vendor. He presented a table in front of him full of jars and bowls that had pickles of every color: red, green, yellow, purple, you name it. Decorative painted peppers hung above his head. He had a long gray beard and wore a green turban that complimented his flowing robe that had a gold braided rope holding it shut. He settled in the dim lights of the crowded bazaar.

Nearby at Museyib we led a peaceful existence. Shut in by mud from the heavy rains, we heard rumors about attacks on engineers. They worked on building a railroad in Hilleh to transport grain crops to the capital. Nothing seemed to materialize. The conditions were too weak, to induce the Arabs to raid. One morning while wandering around the gardens on the outskirts of town, I came across some jackals. I took one out with my Webley revolver. It ran, and I fired several times to hit it. When I got back to town, the noise from my gunfire had started a commotion at camp.

At Christmas time, the officer's messes organized their own celebrations. The one we had joined in was mostly of Scottish descent. We asked them to show us how to make Haggis, sheep's pudding, which consisted of whiskey. No one would blame them if it didn't taste amazing, we were happy they had alcohol.

When the weather cleared up. We dashed to Kerbela, a lovely town with miles of gardens surrounding it, and two magnificent mosques. The bazaar was upbeat on this day and had a little of everything. We bought pistachios in bulk, hard to get anywhere else, and various fruits and vegetables. No troops camped in this area, so the prices were lower than usual with reduced demand. We were ordered to go in with armed bands, but I never saw any reason. There was no hostility. The British were remarkable for their tolerance of working with other races and cultures.

They posted Mohammedan decoys as guards on top of the mosques. Only the Muslims could enter the actual courtyard. If not, there would've been disturbances and uproar. Constantinople felt so different. I couldn't put my finger on why, but I guessed it was due to the lack of hostility we felt in Santa Sophia and Jerusalem. The forbidden fruit was always the sweetest. During the guard shift change, a curious Tommy found *Arrick*, a burning liquor distilled long ago, stored in the holiest of mosques, Kerbela. By some sort of miracle, he stole it unnoticed until a few hours later when an uprise began, unbelievers were massacred in the street.

The mosque of Kerbela was blocked because of a clock tower that stood in the center of the courtyard. It was too expensive to cover the tower with a golden scale that shined in the sun. A creative architect papered it with kerosene tins. I imagined that it glimmered at one point, but because of the elements, it rusted with a bluish tint. There were thousands of uses for these oil cans, many utilized by the natives. I thought the best use would be to carry oil from the Standard Oil Company.

A sizable amount of the population living in Kerbela were Indians. The Shiahs were anxious to be buried near

Ali and his sons. They'd frequently request to have their remains transported once they'd passed. The British found this as a convenient way to honor the native rulers' request.

The Lion of Babylon

A dragon on the palace wall

Hilleh is a village in the ruins of Babylon, now a modern town. I didn't get the chance to study those ruins when we went over to the area excavated by the Germans before the war. I believed this was where Balshazzar saw the writing on the wall. The brick walls were built and stamped with cuneiform, web-shaped, ancient characters. In the middle of the drawings was a great stone lion standing over the form of a man. The lion suffered injuries from chips made from Arab rifles in skirmishes. Standing all alone in its majesty, in desolate ruins surrounded by black native tents who lost their whole lives and homes. It gave me a lot to think about. The Babylon ruins were excavated, but who knows if it finished since it was such a small area. The city of Seleucia on the Tigris River was built with brick and masonry. It was brought in from a barge coming from the Babylon ruins through a canal that would be joined by the two rivers.

The prophecy of Isaiah was enforced. Babylon, the glory of kingdoms, was to be as it was when God overthrew Sodom and Gomorrah. Never to be inhabited, nor changed between the generations. No one could pitch a tent, nor were shepherds allowed to use it for folding. Only the wild beasts of the desert were allowed to exist there. The houses were to be full of mournful creatures, such as owls.

A few days after Christmas, we were ordered to return to Baghdad. The trip was going to be rough, but we had a Ford tender to warn us of any soft spots. Once we got to the middle of a bottomless bog, I decided to try it out. It was built as a sound, strong all-enclosed van, like one that carried bread. We turned it over and over until we cleared the mud. Once we got stuck, I went to a nearby Arab village to ask for help. I told what appeared to be a leader of the group that we wanted bundles of brush to put in front of the tires to help with traction. He immediately sent his men out to help us. After getting a good amount of the mud out of the way, I saw one of his wives approach. I thought she was going to head down to help us as well, only to see her wash clothes in a cauldron by the fire. A scene an Arab would never allow in his household happened. His wife refused to move away from us. The Arab yelled in anger. She continued to wash, paying no attention to his fury. When she finished her wash, she said nothing, got up and headed to her nearby hut, and refused to come out. An uncomfortable situation for us to witness, but it seemed to not phase or discomfort her at all. The Arab shook it off and continued on with his business.

After maneuvering and digging, we made it seven miles in fourteen hours on that first workday. By nightfall, we were close to an Arab village. I got a bowl of buffalo milk to use for coffee the next morning. We took off in the early hours of the morning. The trip that day was simpler, and we were in Baghdad by 10 p.m. that evening.

SKIRMISHES ON THE KURDISH FRONT

Before we started off again, we spent a few days making repairs and outfitting. We went to Deli Abbas, Iran, where the Thirteenth Division headquarters was located. This town was in the plains at the bottom of the foothills of the Persian Mountains. It was off of the banks of Khalis Canal, about seventy-five miles northeast of Baghdad. At dawn, we passed through the north gate. Close to where Gen. Maude was buried and made it through the desert. We were thirty miles from Bukuba, an affluent city on the Diyala Banks. From that junction to Kurna, where the Euphrates joined, the most crucial stream on the Tigris.

Sunrise seemed to be one of those bright and shining mornings where you're happy to be alive for another day. We passed several caravans that carried carpets and rugs from Persia. As well as fruits, and veggies from the wealthier agricultural district near Bukuba. The silk manufactured there was of outstanding quality and well-known throughout this country.

Things got rough after we passed through the aerodrome near the town. We struggled to make it through

Deltawa, a village covered in ditches. The rivers flooded, and the lakes and swamps were filled, which we avoided. That night darkness fell in the middle of a network of bogs. We came across an outpost of Welsh Fusiliers and set up camp with them. We smashed one of the bottom plates of our cars, and oil leaked from the crankcase. With our kerosene tins, we patched up the damage and pushed off at sunrise. The route we took wound us through plains, groves of palms, little huts, and a holy man's tomb. I saw plenty of jackals crouched in the distance, or slinking through the groves. Deli Abbas was deserted, it had seen some battle. Turkish planes awaited our arrival.

We trod along and saw the *Jebel Hamrin* "the Red Hills," beyond the snow-covered tips of the Kurdish Mountain Range. A few months before, we'd gone over these same passes to the Jebel, so we made adjustments, and knew exactly what was ahead. We tried to improve a road across the *Abu Hajjar*. The Arabs called it the "Father of Stones" when we were done with it. When allowed, we went on reconnaissance.

We started at daybreak and headed towards a small village called Ain Lailah, which meant the Spring of Night. A lovely name for a tiny cluster of palm trees tucked away in barren foothills. We picked up a surveyor here, an officer who made maps for the Army. We passed countless herds of camels. Some with children perched on their backs. They rattled like sailors on a stormy ship as the camels avoided cars driving nearby. Villages of shapeless black tents filled with nomads huddled in the desolate dunes. We picked up a Turk deserter on our patrol, he'd tried to reach our lines. He said six comrades of his were killed by Arabs. Shortly after, we ran into a cavalry patrol. They escaped over some uneven ground before we could come to terms with them.

Luckily for the deserter, we got to him before they did. He wouldn't have lasted long. We returned to camp at 8:30 p.m. and covered a total of 92 miles in our travels. A solid day's work.

Each section had two motorcycles assigned to them. The Generals called them "Jackals," due to the way they looked when hunting lions. The motorcycle riders rode ahead to get a first look, check out the lay of the land, and find the best route to take. When we got into action, they'd stay back a bit. We'd use them to send messages between the sections and different camps. The best rider we had in our section was a Swiss man named Milson. He was English and Swiss and came from Switzerland when the war started to enlist. When he joined us, he spoke only broken English. You could tell he was intelligent. I'd never before seen such a skilled rider. He got his bike through mud when others would carry theirs, and on top of everything, he kept his cool under fire. Each of us was proud to serve among such an astounding group of men. Corporal Summers drove the car I usually rode in. I'd never seen a better driver with such a thorough understanding of the Kurds. He had a subtle sympathy—a gift few had.

Still in the middle of the rainy season, we traveled lightly. All we brought were 40 lb. tents, like an American Dog Tent. Very low top, able to withstand high winds and rainstorms. They kept us dry. We tried to take care of them and not leave them behind. There was room for two men to bunk in the tower of a Rolls. They could close the tarp over the top to keep the rain from coming in through the smaller gaps. The rest of the men used a communal tent or slept in tenders. The bigger tents in the nearby campsites blew over regularly, but it rarely seemed to happen to us. We spent most of our time in the murky darkness among the torrential downpour. Trying to avoid the soaking wet flaps of falling canvases.

Time stood still when the weather was bad. We were cooped up inside our tents without even a plane to look at. One day, when the going was too rough to use the larger vehicles. I set off in a tender to visit a different section of our battery. Thirty five miles in the direction of Persia, near a town called Kizil Robat. We crossed several fords. A sheet of ice over the water kept things still. I heard shouting, "*Sabash, Sahib*" in their language meant "Well Done," from the onlooking Indians.

When I reached their camp, it was void of any useful information. A few minutes later, a motorcyclist came in with a message that our cars were under fire, a short 25 miles away. I bolted up, loaded any spare men, and eight Punjabis from a local regiment. We reached the scene after a disabled car had been abandoned. I saw the men run away. Some of the Turks were confined to a village 250 yards away, while the rest sat behind tall swampy grass to hide. The abandoned car was unable to turn around because of the horrible terrain. None of the men knew that the village had been occupied and were bogged down at the same time the Turks opened fire. By breaking down in an irrigation ditch, the enemy succeeded in continuously flash-flooding the trapped car. The Turks made it hot for the men to dig out of the car. Bullet holes splattered across the men, hitting the cars. We couldn't tell how many Turks were there.

When night fell, the occupants of the abandoned car saw what happened, and were off to find another one, which they found near the enemy. It was missing all four tires and only had the rims. We decided to stay put until the next day. We had just agreed when one of our bike riders showed up with orders from our brigade commander. We were ordered to return to camp immediately. We were nervous about leaving our cars, but orders were orders. We had to obey.

It was past midnight by the time we made it back to the campsite. We were informed that a small attack was planned for the morning and that we should go with the troops to recover the car we left behind. We were instructed to use artillery horses to drag the car free from the mud. We didn't leave camp until 3 p.m. That gave us time to find reinforcements, an armored car that came from another battery. We were held back behind the more advanced cavalry until daylight. We thought the Turks would've destroyed or stolen our car by now. We were not wrong.

As we came on top of the hill that showed where the car would be, we saw smoke coming from an explosion and men scattering back into the village. We made it through the village with the help of the 21st Cavalry squadron. They'd helped free another car that night. It was a terrible wreck, but we were fortunate enough to tow it. I wanted to speak with the head of the village. I walked toward an isolated cluster of houses a few hundred yards to the left of the busier area. As I got closer, gunfire erupted. I took cover in an irrigation ditch. I changed my mind and headed back. The country was so badly broken, it was impossible to operate vehicles. We towed all cars we found back to camp, rather than drive the functional ones.

Hauling out a badly bogged fighting car

A Mesopotamian garage

We camped in Mirjana, a few miles north of Kizil on the Diyala River. A pontoon bridge was strewn across the river. We were joined by a machine gun company as well as a battalion of native infantry. The river beds were wider than the norm, but being so large it limited the amount of water that went through to the canals for most months out of the year. In the springtime, the floods caused the river to rise and the channels to be more accessible. We'd gotten the cars across the river before it started to rise. That night, part of the bridge was removed or lifted up, making it ineffective. The water continued to rise. Branches and trees swept past us. We made several fruitless attempts to get across these clumsy pontoons, but gave up, retiring back to be marooned. We gave ourselves small rations of sleep and rotating watch until the rain stopped or the river lowered. Whichever came first. If the Turks had any brains at all, they'd have attacked us. Four slow days went by and on that fourth and final day, the river subsided as quickly as it had risen.

We had decent patrolling conditions, and every day we'd make longer treks. Sometimes, we'd run into an enemy and have a small skirmish. We were known for our infantry and ability to maneuver effectively. The enemy set traps for us. They dug holes and scattered loose dirt over them. It was an effective strategy and if we drove into it, we'd be trapped in a deep, dark hole. The closest town from there was occupied by the Turks, Kara Tepe, nine miles away. In this scarce land was a number of small native villages, where the residents led an unpleasant existence. The next morning, Turkish soldiers attacked and fired several rounds at us. We fought to a standstill, using the cars for cover and firing back on them. In the evening, wild Kurds snuck in and killed off injured Turkish soldiers. The Turks accused the Kurds of having shared private information with us. They took hostages and beat them for having met with us.

An older sheik with whom I'd often sit and gossip with asked why we never advanced on his village. His assistant roasted berries for our coffee in the nearby handmade fire. He spoke at length about how he wished the village children could grow to adulthood unharmed.

In this country, Kurdish and Turkish were the most common spoken languages next to Arabic. But names and titles were in the Turkish language. For example, Kara Tepe meant Black Mountain, and Kizil Robat meant Tomb of the Maidens. My spellings of these names differ from more conventional methods, I'm not quite sure I was taught that. At the time, map-makers didn't meet often, so their labels differed with the many translations.

Kizil Robat was a quaint, attractive town. I spent a few mornings wandering around with the mayor, Jameel Bey. A well-groomed Kurdish chieftain of the Jaf tribe. He owned gardens with palm trees, oranges, pomegranates, and figs. Kurds mostly worked on the irrigation ditches, similar to the ones I'd have to hide in. Piles of rags laid in the sun—oh wait, not a pile of rags, but a little boy. I was introduced to Jameel's son. He was white with rosy cheeks, like most American babies.

Harry Bowen, the brother-in-law of Gen. Cobbe, was the

political officer assigned to oversee Kizil Robat. He spoke fluent Arabic and was respected by the natives. His house was a grand oasis. I looked forward to our fine dinners and intelligent conversations. The town was small but had three Turkish bathhouses. One belonged to Jameel, but judging by the children and babies clogging the entrance, it was for staff and family. We went to another with an older Persian who understood the art of massage. A fantastic feeling after a hard day's work of battle and repairing cars.

In late February, we passed through Kizil Robat with our former Russian allies. They were Cossacks, a good-looking lot as they rode their horses, but the ponies were unkept and small. When Russia withdrew from the war, they asked permission to continue fighting by joining our battery. They had no regard for discipline. It was difficult to keep them under control, as well as stop them from pillaging the natives.. When the Russians first established a connection with us, some armored cars were sent out to bring back the Cossack General Leslie. We were surprised to learn he spoke no English whatsoever. Apparently, his ancestors were from Scotland and was in the court of Peter the Great.

ADVANCING UP THE EUPHRATES

In early March, we got orders to return to Baghdad. The armored cars were going to be used in an attack on the Euphrates Front. There was a lot of speculation on what our mission exactly was. Some claimed we were going to breakthrough to establish a better connection with Gen. Allenby's forces in Palestine.

The war effort in France called for a reduction in Eastern forces. Now, we had to wait until October instead of March as originally planned. Spring would've been ideal to venture up the Euphrates. And more practical to cross the desert by vehicle via the Tadmor connection, which joins Syria and Mesopotamia.

When we advanced, the roads were rough, and rain poured. We couldn't wait any longer. We were ordered to attack. We needed to salvage what we could, separate the essentials, and tread our way through the mud. It was a slow and dreary process, but we managed to get to Bukuba by sundown. The river rose during its predictable and periodic floods. We were lucky to find a pontoon bridge built a half hour before we got there. No one could tell how long this flood would last, but the river was rarely known to go down in under a week. At that time, the trains and railroads only went as far as Bukuba. We crossed the river using a wooden trestle. I loaded motors on a flatbed and got them across the Diyala River that way.

After making arrangements to get this done, I wandered toward the bazaar to get something for dinner. In the native fashion, I bought a loaf of bread from an elderly woman and then headed to the pickle booth to pick out some beets to wrap in my bread. I went over to the meat stop and picked up some roasted lamb-kabobs. The meat was cut up into rectangles, seven inches long, and placed on top of burning charcoal. Inside the shops were long bench-like tables for the customer to organize his recent purchases, or eat his meat kababs. Afterward, he'd head to the coffee houses to have more than one cup of tea, and a few cups of coffee to top it off. The Arabs seemed to rarely eat. When I did see them eat, they gorged like it was their last meal.

The next morning, we loaded up the cars and started off via train to Baghdad, 30 miles away. Railroads wound throughout the desert. Water tanks were scattered here and there, always with a native regiment guarding them. We stopped at one particularly desolate area. A young officer ran up to us and asked if we'd have tea with him. We agreed, and he brought us back toward the tent where everything was ready and laid out. The poor guy was barely over 20 years old and looked lonely and homesick. Many younger officers wounded in France were sent to India. They'd help train and get acclimated to the ways of the Indian Army, while healing up and recuperating. This officer had only been out of the country for a month. Ten days before that, he led the Sikh company on guard duty.

We spent a few days in Baghdad to compose ourselves while our cars were sent to be painted camouflage to resemble supply trucks. We took every precaution to prevent the Turks from noticing that we had mass grouped for an attack. The night before our assault, a message came that a political officer at Nejef was executed, and the town was in revolt. We were instructed to send a section out there immediately.

Lt. Ballingal and his team were chosen while the rest of us prepared to join them with another wave of troops the next morning. The first part of the planned route was through the desert to Fallujah. An agricultural and prosperous town on the Euphrates River. The railhead laid beyond an area known as Tel El Dhubban, or "Hill of the Flies." From there, we used the Arab barges, called *shakturs*. We crossed over the river by taking a bridge of boats and continued along the bank to Ramadi. This is where I stayed, instructed to help escort the army commander on a tour of inspection.

The small towns along the Euphrates were more visually pleasing than the ones on the Tigris. This area was more developed with inviting gardens surrounding the villages. The village of Hit laid 20 miles upstream of Ramadi, by far the most beautiful. Ancient and built on top of a hill, with one of the best views of the river. Not a spec of green, but stood out harshly in comparison to the palm groves that lined the river bank. Nearby bitumen oil deposits were a focal point for the town center. The jars the women used to extract water from the river were made of wicker instead of copper or metal. The smell of the burning oil and Sulphur was horrid. The residents of the village argued this is what saved their town from cholera epidemics. We'd captured Hit a few weeks before. The planes flying low reported that the awful smell was due to the dirt and filth, which we all knew to be false. "Eyewitness" was the local official newspaper and mentioned it in the articles. As I passed through town, the residents apologized for the smell.

A water-wheel on the Euphrates

After taking our army commander back to the railhead, we retraced our steps the eight miles back to Hit upstream, guiding us toward Syria. The road after passing through Hit was in terrible shape. The engineers worked on it day and night to keep it open and partially functional. In the attack we planned, we were ordered to take off to Syria, where our armored cars were assembled. Our camp was near a Turkish hospital.

Stars and crescents were placed to signal our airplanes when to start dropping bombs. One of the two crescents was made out of limestone and turf. The batteries took turns going on reconnaissance. They came in for a good deal of crossfire and explosions. The road was unpleasant since our camels and other transport animals were killed on their routes during the Turkish retreat from Hit. We never saw jackals or vultures coming to feed on carcasses. After scoping out the enemy's positions, progress, and defenses, we took the longer route back to camp.

One early morning, I went to an island off of the river. The cool, calming appeal attracted me the day we arrived, it fulfilled its promise. The only place I came across in Mesopotamia that had a surviving fragment of the Garden of Eden. Almost a mile long, and scattered along it were eight thick-walled houses. The whole island was a vast, palm tree grove. Filled with pomegranates, apricots, oranges, figs, and grapevines that grew beneath the palms. The grass on the ground speckled with blue and pink flowers. I found fields of wheat, irrigation, and water ditches propelled by giant water wheels, thirty to fifty feet wide. Described in the bible, it seemed they weren't modified since. I saw as many as fifteen in a row. As the wheels scooped up the water, it created a waterfall into the gourd-shaped jars bound to the sides and near the bottom. Once filled to the rim, they pulled on the wooden axles.

On the night of March 25th, we got word an attack would take place the next morning. Our cars were ready to move out at 3 a.m. before the sun rose. Since midnight, we saw shadowy figures pass through to get into forward position. One of our batteries went with infantry to advance against the defensive positions at Khan Baghdadi. The rest of us went with the cavalry to cut off the Turks at the flank if they tried to retreat upstream.

We were well on our way by the time daybreak came. The country was broken up by river beds and ravines. We knew it would be a long and rough march ahead, especially with the poor quality of maps we had. A German officer we captured had gotten a hold of our most updated map, which included a large ravine we'd missed on the last version. This convinced us that any new movements we'd attempt would be a failure. We advanced down the Nullah riverbank, which would've taken us to Khan Baghdadi instead of ten miles north of it, as we'd hoped. With the help of our airplanes, we were set on the right path. I was in charge of the men and vehicles carrying supplies and spare tires. I spent most of that day in the leading caravan. Once in a while, I'd go into an armored car and check out some of the separate missions. The Turks had anticipated getting flanked and shot at us.

That afternoon, we turned toward the river. Our cavalry was immediately engaged. The terrain was far too broken up for our cars to move effectively. At nightfall, we laid down next to the cars and were soon off to sleep. At midnight we woke to the sound of whizzing bullets pinging off of the rocks near where we slept. A night attack was underway. It gave us a special eerie feeling. We guessed that the Turks would retreat from Kahn Baghdadi and ran to our battery's outposts. In a few short minutes, we returned gunfire with the same intensity. The ripping of the machine guns on both sides were nonstop. Our enemies underestimated us, because without too much of a fight, they surrendered. Not long after we took 1,200 prisoners. The cavalry made a temporary prison camp so we could catch a little more sleep before the sun came up.

At dawn, we came across another section of 2,000 enemy Turks. They retreated a short distance away until we started moving at daylight, then they surrendered. Within that group were several German officers. They were well equipped with machine guns and long rifles. Their tools and medical supplies were mostly Austrian made, as were their portable kitchens. We took stock of what and who we'd captured. We received word that Khan Baghdadi held many prisoners. We were instructed to push on and take over Haditha 30 miles to the north. Everyone hoped we could recapture Col. Tennant, who was last in command of the Royal Flying Corps in Mesopotamia. He was shot down at Kahn Baghdadi the day before the last attack. We learned from our prisoners that he'd been sent upstream, on his way to Aleppo. Rumor was he was held in Haditha or a surrounding village.

Enemy troops had gotten between us and the river and had made their way back to a functional road. We pushed on with little opposition, except for occasional groups of stragglers who tried to stay hidden behind rocks and sniped at us, with no luck. We disarmed them and they surrendered. We directed them to walk backward until they were recovered by our cavalry. The scene reminded me of hell. The road was covered in scattered equipment and dead and decaying Turks. Hard to believe the wounded could survive as the heat increased—the dead were better off.

We reached the hills that overlooked Haditha to discover the batteries were in full retreat. Most left the night before. The men that remained opened fire on us, but half-heartedly, and didn't inflict any damage. Many of the town residents lived in burrows between the hills. These burrows were filled with shell casings, casualties laid everywhere. We pushed on and tried to save as much material as possible. We were anxious to keep anything written about the Arabs, so we could check on them. We needed to keep track of our allies and enemies. We recaptured a good amount of medical supplies and more ammunition taken from our forces during the last Gallipoli campaign.

The town of Haditha was 35 miles from Khan Baghdadi, and Ana is the same distance farther from there. We decided to push toward a large bridge on one of our maps, 8 miles this side of Ana. We were to secure that area before the Turks destroyed it. Then cross over to the other side where a temporary camp was set up. The road was in better shape than the last we had seen. Many of the smaller bridges were newly made. We figured out our map was inaccurate. Our planes did a lot of damage to the Turks. As we started to catch up with the bigger groups of cavalry, we had sharp engagements. The desert Arabs hovered like vultures in the distance. They waited for darkness and camouflage to loot.

That night we made camp near the bridge. At dusk, the Red Cross ambulances and some straggling cavalry caught up. The cavalry had a rough couple of days. The men had little to eat and even less for the horses, but somehow they pushed on and got to us. They were the 7th Hussars. We'd recovered one of their sergeants who'd escaped from the

Turks. He'd covered 40 miles on foot, and the Turks had treated him alright. The Turks were good, clean fighters. Our officers were treated well, as long as one of us had something to share. With the enlisted men, they were less considerate.

I believed it was because the Turks didn't worry much about the welfare of their troops. This made them not care much for ours. The Turkish private thrived on the starvation of our men. The attitudes of their officers were amusing yet exasperating. They took food and supplies for granted, knowing they would be treated with the conditions of an honored guest. They were bitter, and complained about not having enough coffee, even though we survived without it.

We had no source of supply. The German prisoners were known to cringe when captured. Once they discovered they wouldn't be ill-treated, they became arrogant. We had recovered men that had been captives. One Tommy from Manchester, taken before the fall of Kut, escaped and lived among the Kurd's tribesmen for seven months, before finding his way to us. Many Indian prisoners were sent off to work on the railway construction that connected Berlin to Baghdad. But they escaped between Nisibin and Mosul and struggled to join our lines.

It was a relief when the Red Cross supplies came in, and we could give them to the wounded. Throughout the night, they transported medical supplies back and forth to the main evacuation camp out at Haditha.

By the time the sun rose that morning, we were off again. In the dark night, the Arabs pillaged the abandoned supplies. In some cases, they killed the wounded Turks. The animals used for transport by the enemy, as well as their horses, were in terrible shape. The wet winter months made it difficult to bring in enough supplies. Due to the cold, the roads settled so deep into the mud that they were impassable. After another look at the map, we found that instead of being 8 miles from Ana, we were actually 17 miles.

We still made it without any serious hurdles. The town was beautiful and covered in gardens that lined the riverbanks for five miles. Besides palms and fruit trees were great olives—the first I'd seen in Mesopotamia—and rare almond trees.

The majority of the enemy's troops had vacated the town. Still, we captured the Turkish governor and a good amount of their garrison. Including many that had escaped from Haditha. The disaster left at Khan Baghdadi was only reported the day before, we'd cut all the telephone wires. The Governor didn't believe we'd made it as we did. He spent most of his life in Hungary and only had a few months' notice of our advance. The prisoners we took in Haditha had different opinions on when the commander of the air forces would make their next move.

Our cars were ordered to look for a colonel as long as we had enough fuel to get him back. Captain Todd of the Eighth Battery was leading his men 30 miles north of Ana, when they caught a glimpse of a herd of camels surrounded by horsemen. A few belts from the machine gun shooters scattered the group. Col. Tennant and his mate, Major Hobart, were safe and sound in the back of one of our caravans.

We heard from our Turkish captives that a large golden convoy would be sent back from Ana. Some said that one or two days before our arrival is when it was planned. The supply of fuel we'd brought was almost gone, we needed to find more to continue our pursuit. The man in command of the armored car sector was Major Thompson. He had me take the tenders back as far as possible to find an oil dump and draw 1,000 gallons, since that's what the tender could carry.

I emptied all the trucks and loaded them with wounded soldiers and prominent prisoners and the Governor of Ana. He was a knowledgeable, middle-aged man who didn't speak any Arabic, but fluent French. Mid-afternoon, we started off again, I had no idea where to find more fuel. On our way, we were shot at by Turks who hid in the hills. A small but determined force halted their cars in scattered places on the curvy road. Large boulders littered the hills above us and could've been pushed down on top of us. Luckily, no one had that idea.

Upon retracing our steps for a good 60 miles, I got word an enemy patrol dump was discovered by our men. A special airplane supply the colonel and his infantry guarded. We were instructed that none of it should be used for vehicle fuel. He cooperated with me, but refused to read the letter I brought. He allowed me to load up my tenders. The attack batteries were well prepared and highly regarded. We encountered them many times. They met us halfway and helped us often in tough situations.

By the time we got everything ready for our trip back, it was after dark and everyone was exhausted. I managed to find tea, but no sugar or milk. The strong, steaming brew washed down the skimpy supply of the cold beef we had for dinner. It was a star-lit night, but not bright enough to make out the ditches in the road. After we'd left, we ran into a few armored cars instructed to bring back rescued aviators once they had been outfitted again and supplied.

During our stop, my sergeant found out about an emergency run station. An older and experienced sergeant could always hold his liquor. He saved it for times such as these when it would be of great value.

I had been driving all day long and had a tough time staying awake. I dozed off twice. The first time I sprung awake was from a car starting over the embankment. The second time was after a huge rock rolled at me from the road. We crept back into Ana at close to 2 a.m.

PURSUIT OF THE GOLD CONVOY

Our plan was to capture a gold convoy at 4 a.m. This gave us a whole two hours to sleep. I curled up in the back of a Rolls Royce that was pulled off the road. Through the morning dew and mist loomed the outlines of an armored car parked a little ahead of me.

Captain Carr of the 13th Battery was in command of this expedition. Unless someone was shooting or we were in an area under machine-gun fire, the officer and his NCO stood behind the turret. They held themselves using leather loops bound to the sides.

Our toolboxes attached to both sides of the trucks and served as good seats on the longer runs. When we were engaged by gunfire, the crew got inside and pulled the steel doors closed. The slits shut on the driver and passenger sides when the firing was more substantial. We had peep-holes on either side, and on the back end that could be closed, like the back of a pick-up truck. There was an area to slide a gun out on most sides that could be shut when not in use. Sections of men would come in and try to shoot into the small openings. One of our drivers was shot in the head in that exact fashion near Ramadi.

The bottom of the car was made of wood, the bullets ricocheted up through them. If we'd used steel, it would've made the car too heavy. The large gas tank in the back of the truck was protected by steel plates but still vulnerable. A reserve tank held ten gallons inside of the turret. We often had issues with the fuel lines during the hot days. It made the turret feel like a sauna and the pedals so hot they'd burn your feet.

Forty miles north of Ana, we arrived at a large Khan roadhouse. These houses were built along the main roads. Their design was simple. Four walls, two tiers, rooms and booths built-in. An enclosed court where the camels and horses would rest for the night. As a whole, the area was built strong, but the roads were limited to the desert tribesmen. As we drove toward a large gate, we heard loud voices from a group of Jewish and Armenian merchants that had taken refuge there. Some of them left Ana toward Aleppo before hearing about the fall of Kahn Baghdadi reached that village.

Others were killed by the Turks when they heard about our advance. They seemed to all be plundered by the Arabs. Some of the cargo animals ran off from the gunfire. This made the merchants powerless, unable to move. The women cried out and called for help, children tumbled over the confused mounds of merchandise. Some Armenians had connections in Baghdad and were able to transmit bits and pieces of information. Everyone begged for permission to go back to Ana and then the Capital. We had no means of transporting that many people, and any attempt was out of the question.

Once we got a few miles further, we discovered Arab

troops making their way inland a mile or so away from us. We watched them over the ravines. They had stolen camels that looked in bad shape. Two of our cars made a failed attempt to reach them, but not before we received a few shots from their machine guns.

We caught up with a band of Turks, as well as several isolated stragglers robbed by the Arabs. Usually, they'd surrender without hesitation. We disarmed them and ordered them to head back toward Ana. Often we'd run into Turkish cavalry. I rode with the Ford tender and a few supplies. The ground was broken up and nearly impossible to maneuver. When a tire would blow out, I'd jump down and be ready to replace it. The armored cars had a head start, and we rushed to catch up with them. During my hurry, I failed to notice they left in pursuit of a cavalry troop.

We got to a large building that the Turks used as barracks. I made sure I'd seen there were cars there before me, careful not to approach the enemy. I found my troop and we drove up to the door. I jumped out of the car and shoved it wide open. Inside of that yard was cavalry. I only had my Webley revolver in my belt holster. There was nothing I could do other than put out a strong front. I shouted in Arabic to the one in command. I ordered them to surrender as if our forces had surrounded them when it was just me. They appeared to have been just as surprised and surrendered immediately, turning the post over to me. Elridge, our Ford driver, took the rifle the Turkish commander had strapped to his side. Then we made our rounds with our captive as an escort.

One of the hospital wings was a post we used, and under the direction of a small but knowledgeable Armenian doctor. He asked the universal question, "When would

Great Britain free their own country, and would it become an independent state?"

There was a limit to the number of prisoners that we could transport back with us. I offered a spot to the doctor since he'd be helpful for obvious reasons. When I offered, his response was going to his trunk and getting a picture of his wife and young daughter. They were stuck in Constantinople, and he hadn't seen them for two years. He thanked me but declined in hopes of seeing his family again.

Once the cars were ready, we set off in pursuit of the gold convoy. We couldn't seem to get accurate information about its conditions. Some said it was running behind, others said ahead, but we didn't give up. It could've been concealed in a ravine off one of the roads we'd passed. Short of Abu Kemal, a town in Syria off the Euphrates, we captured three Germans. They were terrified when we took them. Once they'd calmed down they explained their fear of getting shot. Once we started to treat them well, they had to be set in their place.

A "Red Crescent" ambulance

During our run back to Ana, we picked up a few more prisoners. Twenty-two was as many as we could handle. I ran one of the larger cars, it handled easier than I expected with the added weight of armor plates. We took great pride in the cars we rode in. We'd usually name them. In the

Fourteenth section they had Silver Dart, Silver Ghost, as well as Grey Terror and Grey Knight. The car I rode in met its fate a few days before the armistice, long after I went to France. It was hit by two direct shots from an Austrian 88.

We got back to our camp at Ana a little after midnight, right in the palm gardens. Although we didn't succeed in capturing any gold convoy, we did get many valuable prisoners and other items. I found papers that used to be owned by a German political agent we'd captured. They contained information about the Arab situation. They all but proved the Germans were the ones instigating the murder of a political officer at Nejef. An excellent addition to those papers were letters addressed by Arab sheiks directed to the Kaiser. They thanked him for iron crosses they were awarded. I bet there were underlying sarcasm in these letters. They were Mohammedan Arabs that withstood the Holy Land of the Christian invasion.

When we arrived at Ana, we got orders to evacuate the following morning. They were prepared to blow up the ammunition dump, a series of buildings that were all connected. We warned the inhabitants and told them to hide in caves along the hillsides. Our troops went back to the same camp we occupied near the bridge the night before we got to Ana. In the afternoon, Major Edye turned up. He was a political officer traveling only with an Arab attendant. His attendant would pitch camp for the Major, which consisted of a saddle and a blanket right beside our camp. He was a fascinating man with a real knack for languages. In only a year, he learned the modern language Abyssinian while traveling through Abyssinia. There was a famous Orientalist with the Germans that he corresponded with before the war. He'd mailed the Major a letter at the outbreak of the war, written in ancient Abyssinian.

The main explosion was set to be followed by smaller ones, with longer and longer intervals between. This lasted throughout the night. General Cassels, who commanded the cavalry brigade, asked to return to Ana the next morning to check on the recovery of the destroyed camp. We agreed this was fine, and he took an escort of armored cars. I was the only one that spoke Arabic in the batteries, so my services were requested. As we got to town, a rattle of small guns peppered the sky around us. They sounded more like fireworks. The General noticed I had a Polaroid camera and asked me to go to the dump and take pictures. I swallowed my fear and inched my way around the edge of the dump trying to get a good angle. As I made my way back, a shell exploded. We quickly moved our cars.

I went to the mayor's house to see how the town looked after the explosions. The mayor was a solemn old Arabian man. He showed me the damage the shells had done with no expression on his face. The surrounding houses were riddled, but the natives followed our warning and hid. They didn't suffer any deaths. After a cup of coffee with the Mayor in his magnificent garden on the river, I came back, and we rode into Haditha. We were supposed to stay there for a week to allow for transporting any captured supplies.

So far we'd had decent luck with the weather. But now the rain started. We crawled underneath our cars with blankets. We took all the precautions we could, but it didn't matter once the hurricane hit at midnight. A wave pushed me out from under my car. I'd found a deserted hut earlier, that I'd marked before dark. I fought against the onslaught of water to make my way there. Although abandoned by the Arabs, they left traces of their previous occupancy. Still, I preferred that shelter over the rainstorm. That roof was airtight.

The entire next day, that storm continued. The Wadi Hauran was a large ravine that led back into the desert for 150 miles. That ravine became a boiling pond of water. When the storm ended, and we crossed over, it dried up. An artillery truck with a heavy anti-aircraft gun was shredded to bits from the hurricane. We wondered what had survived of our rations and feared further supply would be out of the question.

I was the only member of our brigade that spoke enough Arabic to be of good use. It was on me to meet the town's mayor on a long island. We took a ferry across in barges. The native methods were simpler, they inflated goatskins, stripped down, and held the goatskin with one hand, and paddled with the other. They started at the top of the island and reached the shore on the opposite end. Their elder bobbing heads and greybeards looked ridiculous while stripping down nude and trying to inflate the skins.

The mayor proved to be both an intelligent and agreeable man. The food supply was scarce, he didn't offer us any serious help food wise. We made an area in the guest house where we sat cross-legged on pillows in a circle. In the middle, a servant roasted coffee beans with a large shoveling spoon. The desert Arabs seemed to always be held in the highest regard by the kinsmen of their town. It was general knowledge that the elder men of Haditha were an unusually good-looking group of men. We received a few eggs, a delicacy to eat after some black tea and canned beef.

My shoes were destroyed a few days before I took a pair from a Turk who had no more use for them. They were too big and wide, but I was excited to have my own pair of shoes. Even in the machine-gun service they value the importance of their shoes. I was as eager for a meal as I was for those shoes. My supply of reading material was light. I only had *Tancred* by Disraeli. I found myself unable to be empathetic to the character's feelings, while on a French voyage from Baghdad to Aleppo in the year 1808. The author was a cousin of the Great Jean Jacques and belonged to a family known for being Orientalists. Born in Persia and married to the daughter of the Dutch consul, he was equipped for a diplomatic career that awaited him in the East, as well as North Africa. The folks he met with and the remains he found were well thought out and detailed. The river towns had changed little in the last 100 years. The sketches in the book looked like they were drawn yesterday.

Three days after the rise of the waters of Wadi Hauran, they finally subsided enough for us to cross. I got orders to return to Baghdad. The rain brought a change throughout the desert since we passed on the way up. While making the journey, the words of Paterson, the Australian poet, repeated in my head:

"For the rain and drought and sunshine make no changes in the street, In the sullen line of buildings and the ceaseless tramp of feet, But the bush hath moods and changes, as the seasons rise and fall, And the men who know the bushland they are loyal through it all."

The dry desert floor was covered in soft green with heaps of tiny flowers, all delicately fashioned. I saw poppies, daisies, buttercups, and forget-me-nots. While I admired these flowers, the rain started again. This time, we decided to push through and make our way to Baghdad before the road would again become impassable.

SKETCHES OF BAGHDAD

I never spent long periods in Baghdad, four or five days out of each month. In this city, life was complicated and exciting. We were the most foreign of people, but that barrier was never as obvious as one would think. I had many opportunities to mingle with the natives. I met Oscar Heizer, part of the American consul. He had been in the Levant for 25 years, most of which in Constantinople.

After the outbreak of the war, he was stationed at one of the leading ports of the Black Sea. He witnessed terrible massacres. Herds of pitiful people pushed inland to die of starvation. Quiet and unassuming, he acted with speed and agility to help with supplies. He became a universal favorite with both the natives and the foreigners.

I went with him on a ferry across the river to get some tea with the Asadulla Khan, part of the Persian consul. The house had three wings built around a garden, the far wall faced the river bank. The courtyard was an organized jungle of blossoming fruit trees filled with birds singing in tune—without stopping. We sat in the garden and sipped sherbet while cracking nuts and eating salted watermelon seeds.

An array of coffee, sweets, whiskey, and scotch were served. The Koran's rules against alcohol weren't observed by most of the population. Even those who didn't drink in public rarely abstained when alone. Only the extreme conservatives would obey the prophet's commands. They mostly lived in smaller towns.

We inhaled the smoke in the shade of the trees while watching the boats sail by. The maple and palm trees swayed in the wind. The boats were called *gufas*—built like the coracles in ancient England. Shaped round like a basket, with a slight pitch. No Anglo-Saxon would pass them without thinking of the nursery rhyme. "Some wise men of Gotham went in a sea..."

These gufas were about 25 feet wide and carried a variety of things: men, women, cattle, and sheep. The job of propelling a gufa was an art. It spun without moving in either direction. The natives used long, rounded-edge paddles to make good time crossing the river. A crossing was a democratic event. Especially when women returning from the markets had strings of chickens slung over their shoulders.

The profile of Asadulla Khan reminded me of an Incan idol from Peru. Among his several scribes were men of culture focused on Persian literature. Sadi and Hafiz were held far superior to Omar Khayyam. I used many channels to get a manuscript of the Persian-English Rubaiyat. All I could get was a lithograph copy that didn't have a location or date of publication. Only a passing remark about having been printed in the cold winter months. I was told the writings of Omar were regarded as immoral. They were not to be brought into a religious household. My Persian friends would always quote from *Rose Garden* and dig into the raptures of its beauty.

Beneath the consulate was a landing space where our servants carried lanterns as a signal they were ready to be picked up. They'd call this ordeal "*Abu Bellam*" until a boat would appear. The term "Abu" always amused me, since the literal translation is "father." The bazaars owners were known as "father" of whatever wares he had for sale. An old fat man who sold porous earth jars was named "Abu hub," which meant the "Father of water coolers."

My best native friend was Hamdi Bey Baban, a Kurdish chief. His father was captured and sent to Constantinople. After he lived there for several years in partial captivity, he was poisoned. Hamdi wasn't allowed to go back to Kurdistan until he was a grown man. By that time, he'd forgotten nearly all his native language. He spoke and read both French and English. He was granted permission to live in Baghdad as long as he stayed out of the Kurdish Hills.

Hamdi decided to go anyway. He'd arranged for a car driven by a French chauffeur. Gas was sent ahead, dropped at points along his route by camel. The journey was doomed from the start. The villagers had never seen a vehicle before and thought it was a demon. The villagers threw stones. Hamdi was mobbed and nearly killed. He escaped by driving into the crowd at full speed.

His life in Baghdad was volatile. Once, he was arrested and taken back to Constantinople before the British advance. This put his life in grave danger. He didn't care for the Turks and staked everything on an Allied victory.

Hamdi intended to write a book on his family's history. He purchased books and manuscripts for research material. In the East, many well-known history excerpts existed in only manuscript form. They made copies by using scribes. This was common with wealthier men that wished to build a personal library. Hamdi had men transcribe rare chronicles about his family's past. He showed me a passage from a long manuscript in Persian. It told of an execution and 17 beheaded bodies.

I'd also gossip, play dominoes, and drink coffee with my Arabic friend Abdul Pasha. An older man and faithful ally to the British through many trials and tribulations. The dinners at his house on the river were like feasts you'd read about in ancient history. Course after course, without a schedule or plan announced. Each course was the size of a meal in itself, and always more. True to Arabic custom was a rule that the son of the house wouldn't sit down the same time as his father. Before and after dinner, the son chatted and smoked with us.

A jeweler's booth in the bazaar

I had several Armenian friends. Most were related to each other, a parent or sibling, with another family member among the Turks. Several Armenians were attached to highly regarded families. Many held government positions in Constantinople. The secretary of treasury was typically Armenian.

I often dined with one family at the usual Oriental feast.

Dinner varied between Arab or Turkish food with featured dishes. Everyone but the grandmother spoke French. The daughters had a good understanding of literature. They read English books with French translation. The house was furnished with colorful rugs, and generations-old silverware. The youngest generation would play bridge. Since they were all girls, they dressed in their most elegant European fashions. Where they got these clothes was a mystery. Maybe they made them. Nothing had been brought in since the war. Foreign clothes of that grade weren't stocked, only imported. The evenings were enjoyable, so different from my daily life. These three Armenians were the only women I could speak and laugh with in proper fashion.

I'd made friends with another educated and well informed Arab named Père. He edited the Arabian newspaper. His entire life he worked toward building a library and gathered rare books throughout Mesopotamia and Syria. Before the British took Baghdad, the Germans pillaged his book collection. They sent the most valuable to Constantinople or Berlin and sent the rest to their troops. The soldiers made several bonfires, others traded books at the bazaars for supplies. When Père spoke about the ransacking of his house, he was worked up in a white heat of wrath and fury. His eyes flashed as he cursed the vandals who'd destroyed his treasures.

In Baghdad, I met Major E.B. Soane, he wrote, *Through Mesopotamia and Kurdistan in Disguise*. He was born in southern France to a French mother and an English father. His father crossed the US from ocean to ocean in the early 1840s, so he was born with an adventurous spirit. As a boy, he went to work in the Bank of the Angelo-Persians. He took an interest in Persian language and literature. He spent most of his time in the British Museum to translate and catalog Persian manuscripts. He became interested in the Kurds. He spent many years among them to learn their customs and dialects while joining in their raids.

As soon as we settled in the Kurdish Hills, Soane was sent to oversee the newly-captured territory. His quarters were at Khanikin, 25 miles from Kizil Robat, not far from the Persian frontier. One morning, I took a boat across the river to see him. The clouds towered above white snowy peaks against a deep blue background. The brightest sky I'd seen in years. The road wound around the empty foothills. A vast grove of palm trees with houses peeked through, divided by a river lined with seven bridges. I made my way through the narrow street, dodging ragged Kurds. I came to a house with a large courtyard decorated with an array of Kurdish men armed with every weapon imaginable. Soane administered a stern but tactical plan for justice. He understood how to handle these men.

The district suffered in fear. Occupied by a rotation of Turks and Russians before we took it over. This caused the natives to be robbed without mercy. Thousands of them were starved to death.

During my time in Deli Abbas, groups of starving men came through begging for work or food. Soane had a khan that sat on the outskirts of town. He transformed it into a poorhouse where he'd put starving women and children that drifted in from all over Kurdistan. A scary assembly of the thinnest people I'd ever seen. As some women were fed and became stronger, he turned the Khan administration over to them. He divided them into groups and monitored which groups were fed and when. They got healthier over time and helped clean up the village. The Kurds had a lot of self-respect. I understood the admiration and enthusiasm Soane had for them.

In Baghdad, you either lived in a cellar or a housetop. They called cellars "serdabs," a large chimney shaped to withhold the high winds but with enough ventilation to breathe on the hot desert days. We slept on rooftops, even ate there at times. The town was headquarters for the Expeditionary Force. We'd always run into a friend, or at least an acquaintance.

Meetings were held at horse tracks. Each participant sent a representative, and Arabs joined these meetings. A wild tribesman took a significant lead in the race by taking off his cloak and shouted chants of triumph. The Arab that came after him was less enthused and handled the business in a more professional manner. His horse wasn't as quick as the others. The energy at these horse tracks were grand. Radiant colors, silky hooded cloaks bright enough to see across the crowds. From my rooftop, the colorful abas made the crowd look like a poppy field.

In Samarra, an amusing incident took place with a few officers' wives captured at Ramadi. The Army commander didn't want to ship them to India and Burma to be with their husbands. He sent them to Samarra and across the lines, to the Turks. After several messages sent by plane, we left them at an assigned hill and the Turks would come for them. We had quarters arranged for them to be considered somewhat civil. When the wives were brought back to their countrymen, they cried hysterically. We didn't know if it was the Turk's being heartless or not having any use for these specific women. Twenty-four hours later they still stood waiting. We sent them back to Baghdad.

On occasion, I'd go to an Arab theater. The plays were burlesques since the Arabs had a great sense of humor.

Most of the puns were over my head, but there was still plenty of slap-stick comedy understood by most if not everyone in the audience. There was always dancing, while mostly mediocre. One older man was a remarkable performer and would've been appreciated anywhere. The songs were amusing and spirited. The chorus of one of my favorites went "*Haido, Haido, rahweni passa,*" which translates to "I say, I say, show me your pass." Spies had been an issue in the past, everyone showed their tickets upon request. A sign of good faith and this song demanded it.

Captain Lloyd was my companion for many of the meetings with the natives. He was stationed in Burma, then India, for many years. He was an established Persian scholar. I asked him why I'd never seen him drink coffee, in all the coffee houses we visited. He said he'd been poisoned by a cup of coffee once delivered to him.

I looked forward to my trips to Baghdad. It gave me a chance to experience a different life than I was used to. Although it was temporary, it helped me take my mind off the war, and about how the world swirled into hell. Still, as each morning came, I was ready to set off to my next destination. I was as happy to leave the desert as I was to arrive.

ATTACKING THE PERSIAN FRONT

I arrived at headquarters after the attack on the Euphrates. I expected to hear about my transfer to France and receive my orders to proceed there immediately. I intended to join the American Army once it became part of the war. I mulled over the best method to execute my plans. When things looked bad for the Allied forces in March 1918, France was the place to be. General Gillman, a staff chief, had shown himself to be a good friend on several occasions. He told me he could arrange a transfer to France, and once I arrived I could figure out the best way to get into the American Army.

I waited for my orders. The brigade commander of armored cars, Major Thompson, sent for me. He warned me about the action on the Kurdish Front. Only two batteries headed out, the 8th and 13th. I wasn't from either, but he wanted me to come along and command the supply trains. I jumped at the opportunity. The attack promised to be quite interesting.

We were ready to move within an hour's notice. Several days passed with bad weather that held us back. The melting snow from the mountains caused the rivers to rise and flood. The Tigris rose 16 feet overnight. A lower bridge broke and washed away. Everything possible was done to save the upper bridge and reinforce it. Every hour it gave under the strain of the yellow waters.

An elderly Arab man on the river pointed out that one could tell by the color of the water, which rivers came in through the flood. When he saw a new color, he shook his head and said, "This *so-and*-so river is now in the flood. The Tigris will continue to rise."

In the dark of night, we received orders to set out at 6 a.m. the next morning. We were to push through to Ain Leilah. The country had changed since I was there six weeks before. The desert had blossomed. We ran through several miles of clovers, the sweet smell lingered in the air. The smell reminded me of America, I thought of home, family, and the Long Island meadows. The vibrant red poppies kept with the country. We passed Indian cavalry with bright red flowers woven through their dark hair.

We approached the hills. They looked less bleak with a soft green covering the small oasis of Ain Leilah. It no longer stood out as before. The roads were still in good shape. We reached camp at 4 p.m. I set off with one of the tenders to find old friends I knew to be in the nearby regiments. I noticed groups of Arabs I passed played a new game. A stake put into the ground with a rope about 10 feet long. Someone held the end of it with a pile of items and clothing at their feet. The group of Arabs stood around him in a circle. The object of the game was to grab something from his feet before the person holding the string could catch you. They seemed to enjoy themselves, even the old men played along. It was great to see a pleasant side of the Arabs.

We were ready to leave before daybreak. The mission was a flanking maneuver. The direct attack was going to be on Kara Tepe, and if that was successful, we'd move on to Kifri. We were to intercept enemy troop reinforcements and or cut off the garrison's retreat.

In the early hours, the country gave a lovely impression with its green grass and hills peeking over. Miles of daisies with clusters of red poppies scattered throughout. The occasional hollows peeked through with brilliant blue flowers. On the river banks were tons of colorful birds. The most I'd seen in Mesopotamia, the only exception was the vivid green birds In Ana along the Euphrates.

Column marching is slow and dreadful, especially after sunrise in a hot afternoon. We were covered in dust, not a breath of fresh air spared. The miles seemed endless. At noon we stopped alongside a narrow stream known as the Oil River. A common name in this part of Persia where oil supply is heavy. Drinking the water from the river would be deadly. A few miles down, the engineers found a good location to build a bridge across the creek. The main body of water was stopped in an area called Umr Maidan. We were sent over to form a line across the main road that led from Kara Tepe to the Turk's territory.

It was dark by the time we came to the crossing. We treaded along until we came to a road. It was impossible to do anything strategical by choosing a position. We arranged our cars the best we could. In the desert, we were "out in the blue," which described our situation the night of April 26th. We expected we'd hit some traffic going at least one direction, but the night passed without issue.

Indian cavalry bringing in prisoners after the charge

By 4 a.m., we made our way through the darkness. As the sun rose, we became visible to the Turks. They shot at us. We got a message Kitfri was evacuated, and the garrison must fall back to the road that ran parallel to the road we were on. Separated by nine miles of vacant country land. The cavalry caught up to us and pushed off to intercept the Turks by horse. We tried to follow, but it was difficult to dodge the hills and ravines, we made little headway. We stumbled across a road that led us the approximate direction we wished to go.

In early afternoon we caught sight of a large troop of Turks. They marched on the parallel road, winding along the base of the hills. We headed north and tried to intercept them. We put the pressure on, the cavalry joined in from the south. We advanced along the curved roads. The cavalry crossed over and charged forward to the Turks. A rousing scene. The powerful Indians sat on their horses with grace and dignity. Their drawn swords glared in the sun as they came within close quarters of the Arabs. We heard shrieks and screams as they slashed the Turks, along with cries of triumph from the Indians.

The dead and wounded were skilled swordsmen. The battlefield reminded me of the battle books I read as a boy, rather than any other war I had seen in my lifetime. We took over six hundred prisoners, many Turks escaped to the mountains to hide behind rocks and snipe at us. A tenacious bunch. The entire next day while we traveled along the road at the bottoms of the hills, they shot at us from hidden spots where it was impossible to dislodge them.

While the prisoners were brought in, we spotted one of our airplanes crashing. We made our way over to find that neither the pilot nor co-pilot was injured. The climate conditions made flying over Mesopotamia difficult. These planes were designed to work in France during the summer. The heat and dry air warped the propeller blades, and any parts made of wood. This caused dust to get into the machinery when taxiing. Many pilots traveled from France with amazing flying records. They met an untimely death due to not being prepared for these conditions.

One poor guy that set off on a reconnaissance without water and food got lost and ran out of gas. He landed in the middle of the desert. They sent armored cars to search for him. By the second morning, they found his limp body near the camp. He made it far through the night and collapsed and likely died of exhaustion. His clothes were stripped from being overheated, or a robbery attempt. A death of this manor seemed sadder to me than getting killed in combat. The LAM batteries were close with the Royal Flying Corps.

When news came that a plane was downed in the middle of the desert, we posted a printed notice in Arabic, Persian, Kurdish, and Turkish. We let the readers know a reward would be paid to anyone who brought the pilot to the safety of the British lines.

On the night of April 27th, we set up a temporary camp "out in the blue." Once sunlight came, I made my way back to Umr Maidan to search for more fuel. I made a quick trip so I could catch up to the armored cars that were back in action in a field of swampland. The grass was high, the ground soft, it was difficult to do much. A couple of small hills were good vantage points but not missed by the Turks either.

Ten miles from Tuz Kurmartli, the next well-known town held by the enemy now that Kifri had taken over. It was there the Turks retreated when we had cut them off. We were unable to operate as effectively as we wanted. We went to the Kifri-Kirkuk roads to take those to the hills that still had camels and machine guns. We came to a village named Kulawand. It seemed unoccupied except for a single hut with women and children inside. Here we stopped and waited for orders that were to come at nightfall but didn't come on time. I sat underneath a ruined wall and read between my two books until darkness fell.

In the middle of the night, a mix of native and British infantry came up. They had marched for the last few days and were all dressed up, cheerful at the potential attack to come. They still had some fight left in them. The King's Own distinguished themselves and took a strong hold of one of the hills.

At dawn on the 28th, we were underway. We heard reports the Turks evacuated to Tuz, Turkey. We tracked them down and discovered this wasn't true. Not only were they still there, they showed no evidence of leaving. Another small village five miles southwest of Tuz was bitterly contested. Our cavalry had done excellent work and captured a couple of small hills and set up machine guns.

We made our way down the winding road along the foothills. A mile before we got to Tuz, we ran into the Aq Su, a large stream that flowed through a narrow cleft between the hills. The river was low, plenty of spots for us to spread out and make a wide front-line to stop any cars from passing us. I emptied out one of our Ford vans and set out prospecting. I headed upstream toward the mountains but hit a dead-end. I ran into an ancient fort situated at the opening of the gorge that had not been evacuated. Finding a vacant space below us, I barely made it through. I realized it would be difficult for the low-riding Rolls Royce to get through. I worried the flywheel would throw water into the motor. I sent a message back for artillery horses to pull the armored cars across.

While our artillery fire slowed, the Turks had evacuated. I went to see if there were any valuable documents left behind. I drove down, past abandoned artillery in the middle of the road. Several Turkish soldiers came to surrender, I told them to have the Mayor report to me.

When he arrived, I instructed him to take me to the Turkish commanding officer's headquarters. As we drove through the bazaar, everything was closed. Barely anyone walked the streets, I saw a handful of inhabitants peer out from their windows. A good thing the mayor accompanied me, he'd be a valuable hostage. I kept close watch on him. He brought me to a nifty-looking house with solid wooden doors.

An elderly woman came out and ushered us to a large, well-furnished shadowed room with lavish Kurdish rugs. Here I found four young girls. They formed the Turkish General's "field harem." He left in far too much of a hurry to bring them along. They were Kurds and Circassians, and the general seemed to have little taste in his selection of women.

In the tradition of the Garden of Eden, this female group proved to be disastrous to another officer. He heard of my capture and sent me as a priority over field service lines to transfer messages regarding any disposition. Priority wires were sent only on affairs of the utmost importance. When I left the country, my friend was Court Marshalled. I didn't find any documentation of value, so I told the mayor to take me to the ammunition and supply areas. By the time we found them, the cavalry had arrived. I returned to help the cars get across the river.

Once everyone crossed the river, we pursued the Turks. The next town was a muddy, shack-filled town called Tauq, 20 miles down the far side of the river. The cars leading us pushed on once they caught sight of the town. The shooting started right away and came at us the entire time.

The captured Turks were in worse shape than the ones we took on the Euphrates Front. Their shoes were gone, and they looked ragged and malnourished. The length of time to communicate messages had put a strain on them. Supplies came from Nisibin, over 100 miles past Mosul. The country being so broken up made transportation a complicated problem to solve. It was a miracle they fought with as much morale as they did.

THE OTHER MEMBERS of the campaign showed an incredible sense of pride at how our soldiers behaved with the natives. I never heard of a case where anyone was mistreated, man, woman, or child. Minor offenses were committed, but they quickly asked for forgiveness, or someway made right. No doubt a few isolated incidents of some wrong-doings happened since we were a large army. Always bound to be a few bad eggs. But it didn't affect the group's demeanor as a whole.

That night, we camped on the outskirts of Tuz, not far from the British airplane hangars. The next morning, one of the batteries was sent to recon. They took a different route than we did the day before. The commanding officer asked me to join, due to my knowledge of Arabic. The road followed the phone lines, so part of that time we distinguished the countries on either side. As nice as this was, it showed us yet another error on our map. We realized the villages weren't correctly named. Much more recon was called for. In one village, we knocked the corner off of a mud house so we could make a right turn through the narrow roads. The natives were in pitiful condition. The Turks seized their crops and grains. The sheep had been killed, and it was lambing season, so the flocks were smaller than they should have been.

We made our way out of a deep ravine that caused a severe delay. We spotted an attractive town that sat on a steep, flat-topped plain. Once we got deeper into the village, we saw a well-kept gray-bearded Arabic man riding a small gray horse. He informed us he was the leading man in town and how much he hated the Turks. He asked if he could be of any help. I asked him if the enemy had evacuated Tauq, and he replied they did. I was skeptical and asked if he was positive, and he said he could show proof. We followed him, but the trail was rocky, we took our time, and rode side-by-side in what we called a hand-gallop.

We came to a river that flowed in front of the town, it was impossible to get the armored cars across that rough terrain. Our Arabian friend informed us about a usable bridge six miles upstream, but it was too late in the day to make an attempt. We turned back to Tuz and camped. We arranged to meet with a Sheikh in the morning.

The Kurd and his wife

Sheik Muttar and the two Kurds

The next day we found the Sheik waiting for us. We were with him and two other well-groomed Kurdish men. One of them had his wife along with him, saddled on another horse. Together, they guided us up to the bridge. We couldn't confirm whether the road was used for motor cars, we didn't see any in our short time on the bridge. They lived a lifestyle with only men and horses, not thinking about washing out vehicles like we did. We didn't trust the natives with us on our recon missions. We didn't give them too many details of our planned routes. We followed our guides to the bridge. We later found out about another road that would've cut our travel time down by half. We didn't dwell on the past.

When we reached the bridge, it didn't disappoint. Solid and well-constructed. The retreating Turks tried to blow it up. The bombs didn't explode. The damage they intended to cause failed even after six hours of preliminary work. We sent out for engineers and left to clean up in the rapids while we waited. Everyone that wandered around in the wasted places of the world could recall specific memorable swims. Possibly because they'd been on a swim after a long hunt and a weary march. Our dip in the Tauq Chai River took its place as one of my permanent memories.

In the early evening, we headed back to Tuz by car. Our camp was anything but chipper. Starving townsfolk hovered on the outskirts, ready to pounce on anything edible thrown away. Discarded aluminum cans were cleaned out and used as mirrors. Men gave away everything possible so the helpless could ration something from it. News of the starvation spread. Our line of communication traveled far and quickly, it was hard to get much planning or relief work done.

The next morning we crossed over the bridge with few obstacles. Until we tried to make it into town. A couple miles above the main village, a settlement sat on a hill near the popular mosque of Zain El Abidin. Keeper of the mosque is an important position in the community. When he showed himself riding a richly decorated stallion and welcomed us to town, we appreciated being in good hands. He introduced himself as Mustafa, and we took him in one of the Ford vans with us.

It was easier to get the lighter car over the rocky trail than the Rolls. Eventually, one of the fighting cars succeeded in following us. I drove the Ford with Mustafa in the passenger seat. A white horse galloped alongside. The townsfolk sang and shouted, proclaiming our arrival. We stopped at Mustafa's for a cup of coffee and discussed recent events. The information we received proved to be accurate. I brought him into town to help identify the leaders and be sure we got the right people. Our meetings weren't cordial at first. We explained exactly what we were after. Then the mayor became chipper and opened up to us. He had a cheerful face with a big bushy beard. Mustafa told me he was impressed by us and anxious to join forces.

We found bags full of ammunition, supplies, and a walkie-talkie. We were excited about the large number of chickens strolling around. This meant a good supply of eggs nearby. We were honest in paying for what we took and seeing that many men did likewise was impressive. The natives took it for granted when we'd offer to pay them. We used Indian currency, the rupee. A rupee was about 1/3 of an American dollar. All throughout the busier Turkish areas, Turkish currency was welcomed. The natives preferred payment in rupee. We found residents eager to pay in rupees, even in towns like Tauq. The money market in Baghdad was down since a British advance indicated a decline in Turkish exchange. Paper rupees were everywhere and accepted as silver.

Once we arrived back to camp, I learned I was being immediately transferred to the American Army. And to at once report to Baghdad, where I'd be sent to France. Major Thompson asked if I could delay going back until the end of the current advance, a tough decision. The plan was we were going to push on and attack Kirkuk. I requested permission to remain a few days longer to assist in the attack.

On the morning of May 3rd, we moved our camp to the opposite side of the Tauq Bridge. When everything was unloaded, I headed to the gasoline supply in case they called for battle, and had to hurry back. The closest supply allowed to be drawn was the Umr Maidan, 70 miles away. When I reached Tuz, I ran into my friend in charge of the dump site located there. He let me draw whatever I wanted to get back to the bridge before it got too dark.

One car after another had trouble with travel. One with a punctured tire, another with a lost carburetor. They got out tow ropes that snapped on nearly every hill. The car in front of mine's axle broke, and I had to wait until it was moved. To put a cherry on top, a thunderous downpour and hurricane began. The wind blew so hard I felt the car would tip.

What made it worse was the thought of the dry river crossings flooded by morning, holding things up further.

TURKS REFUSAL TO SURRENDER

Two days later, my stay was approved. We marched on a new town called Taza Khurmatli, 15 miles from Tauq. We were to go straight there with no halts. On our way, we heard Taza was occupied by cavalry. We hoped they'd fall back without interrupting our advance.

The cars were out on reconnaissance near this town for the last two days. They'd returned due to artillery and machine gunfire. The Turks had everything ready to stand and fight and not surrender.

In the dim light of dawn, we watched columns of infantry, cavalry, and artillery pass our camp. The Mesopotamian Expeditionary Force were assembled. Steel helmets weren't worn in summer, only winter, due to blazing heat.

The native regiments of British officers wore long tunics with tassels. Just oversized shirts, which seemed to be an adaptation of the native customs. The Gurkhas were supplied with skin-covered helmets, even though they claimed it was unnecessary. The authorities believed a cold front was coming, and the climate change by the

Mesopotamian sun would be brutal. The presence of Indian troops brought on unusual items to the "General Routine Orders" issued by headquarters. One of them referred to a religious festival, written by the Sikhs, and was printed:

> "To our most Dear Brothers now serving the Benign King-Emperor overseas. The chief Khalsa Dewan tenders hearty and sincere greetings on the auspicious Gurpurb of First Guru. You are upholding the name and fame of Gurupurb.
> Our hearts are with you and our prayers are that Satguru and Akalpurkh may ever be with you and lead you to victory and return home safe, after vanquishing the King-Emperor's foes, with honor and flying colors."

The British Empire was loyally served by her Indian subjects, and even more so faithful were the Sikhs.

We let everyone settle for a few minutes before we took off in our vehicles. The trail was wide enough that two-way traffic was allowed without interference. We saw Taza and picked a new sight for camp. The enemy had evacuated town with little resistance. I set off to seek out the local leader and ask him some questions.

In the spring, all the hilltop towns in Mesopotamia were inhabited by flocks of storks. I hadn't seen them in greater force than I did in Taza. On nearly every rooftop, storks threw their heads back and chattered in the unique way that gave them the nickname *Lak Lak* in Arabic. It almost sounded like rattling machine guns. So much so that when I entered the village, I thought Turks were opening fire until I realized what it was. No native would kill a stork, it was considered disrespectful.

The water level was low for the river going into Taza. We managed to get the cars to pass on their own engine power. A few miles down the road was another broad canal that connected to the main river. It turned out it was too deep for the cars, so we had to cross using the artillery horses. The Turks continued to shoot toward the crossings. We pulled back a little, so we didn't get hit, but still had enough assistance to get over.

Once we crossed the river, we made our way around the city of Kirkuk. We needed to get to the road that would lead us to Altun Kupri, a small village inside of Kirkuk. The town, like most others in this part of Iraq, was built on top of the many hills. The Hamawand Kurds were persistent, and a good amount of force was needed to control them. As we came to the road, we saw our cavalry preparing to attack. The Turks put up a stiff resistance, the approaching darkness helped them. After we approached the town, we were ordered to return to an empty village for the night, and prepare to push through early in the morning.

The location of the village was found easily on the map. But it was difficult to locate the exact village they referenced. To make things worse, a storm brewed on the horizon, and the night's blackness settled in. It began to rain. I slept in the front seat of the van for the night, a great idea since it started to downpour at around midnight. I kept dry while many of my companions were washed away. The waterproof flap I rigged withstood the wind and rain and was more gratifying than expected. Bright flashes of lightning showed the dry ravine we spotted was now a roaring, flooded torrent. The water rushed past our cars, half-way up the tires. A large hospital in the field was set up close to the Taza banks. We were told the river rose in such a short amount of time that tents and even ambulances were washed away.

The next morning, the rain turned into a downpour. We figured out that we'd been caught in some of the lowest hills, and that's why the rain was so severe. If it wasn't for the rain, we would have made some good captures. All our cars were bogged down to their axles. No other alternative than to wait for the rain to stop and mud to dry. We had plenty of untouched food and water rations.

Our infantry made their way over at dawn and strutted through the town. The Turks had destroyed the bridge across the Hasa Su. They then retreated to Altun Kupri by following the road from the farthest bank. From a nearby hilltop, we watched everything, powerless and unable to help.

At noon, the sky cleared and the sun came out. We dug out one of our Ford cars to get on the road toward Kirkuk. We discovered the surface was the same weight as the car. We made our way around the outskirts of town, with a few occasional stops to dig a hole or push a car. We were pleased with the number of miles traveled with minimal sunlight to bring the armored cars out of the bog.

Kirkuk

The next morning I set to work on my tenders, even though we had more rain coming that night. We got our cars into Kirkuk. We put them into a well-built facility that had a courtyard we wanted to turn into a garage. The Turks left in great haste, they attempted to destroy anything that they didn't want. They were partially successful.

In my room, I found pamphlets about the American Army. Filled with diagrams and pictures, equipped with several different branches of service. It also included a map of the US showing population by state. The writing was in Turkish. What was the purpose of those flyers?

I found another pamphlet a little more obvious about what it was. Most of the pictures looked to be taken in Sudan showing headless African men. I'm convinced these pictures were from the Armenian massacres. The pamphlet noted it was printed at the Print Press in Kirkuk.

Many great buildings stood like I'd seen in the village. Mostly workshops and armories, but most significant was the hospital. The elongated corridors and deeper windows looked interesting. An up-to-date impression was created from individual patient charts. They had headings for different diseases printed in both Turkish and French. The doctors were mostly of Armenian descent. The residents seemed to all be suffering from starvation and/or dehydration.

I didn't want to go back to Baghdad until I was certain that our troops would not advance to Altun Kupri. Our engineers ran ahead to patch up the bridges to make our cross easier. We followed with the cars to the other side and immediately went on reconnaissance to figure out how strong the town's force was. The bridge was long and could be destroyed from a few locations, but crossing that river would not be an easy task.

The mountains that surrounded us limited our avenues of attack. Altogether it was a tough trek. The Turks were going to make a stand. The Army commander decided to make no further attempts to advance. The recent floods made conditions worse. Our supplies dwindled. It seemed impossible to hold Kirkuk unless materials could be somehow brought in on the rails.

I wandered around the bazaars admiring the oddness. The merchants had closed for one day, but were now open for business as usual. The residents were composed of many different races—mainly Turcoman, Kurd, and Arab. I also saw an array of Syrians, Jews, Armenians, and Chaldeans. The Jewish folk were prosperous. Three languages were spoken here: Turkish, Kurdish, and Arabic. Kirkuk is ancient, but little history was known. The natives pointed out a hill that they claimed to be Daniel's Tomb. Two other tombs belonged to Shadrach and Meskech, as the third part of their trio had been lost. There were many artificial hills throughout the village. In time they'd prove useful for fruit-picking and archaeologist hunting grounds.

The bazaars were filled with all kinds of goods. I got a good price on two rugs and other knickknacks that dated back to the Seleucid times. Many odds and ends for sale in the bazaars were unearthed by Arabian laborers from the desert. I saw gardens built-in truck beds while trading fresh vegetables for our rations. Not many luxuries when living off canned food for as long as we had.

I saw goat heads hanging on house doors. The owners said they were found in the mountains, but were hard to find since few were left. Few large game in all Mesopotamia, the remaining ones inhabited the mountains. I once saw a striped hyena standing not far from me. They were nocturnal animals and said to be common. I'd never seen one until the ruins south of Samarra one evening when riding back to camp. Gazelle were common, and we occasionally hunted one for their meat.

On the plains between Kizil Robat and Kara Tepe, I saw

the biggest gazelles I'd ever seen. Judging by the ancient lions that were painted in the towns, I believed at one time they were plentiful. In the 1840s, Sir Henry Layard spoke of coming across lions quite frequently in the hilly country. Mr. Fogg, a fellow countryman of the same era, wrote a book called the *Land Of The Arabian Nights.* It told of an English captain in one of their steamboats that killed four lions by shooting them from the deck on his boat. He wrote of a meeting close to Hit, where he met a man mauled by a lion and had to go into town to have his wounds tended to. Leopards as well as bears were in the higher mountain regions, while wild boars populated nearby. They inhabited the thickets along the riverbanks. The country permitted pig-sticking as a sport.

Birds used as game were found in all shapes and sizes. Black and gray partridges, geese, duck, and quail. A popular pastime for a week's leave was to go bird hunting. Every type of shotgun was used, from muzzle-loaders bought in the bazaars to the most modern creations sent by mail from India.

After waiting a few more days to be certain an attack would not be ordered, I set out on my return trip to Baghdad. The river at Taza was still high. I borrowed several mules from an accommodating ambulance that helped pull our car across. We took the route that went through Kifri, a clean, stone-built town we found mostly empty. In nearby Kifri were coal mines we'd heard about.

This was the only place coal was dug out from in this country, and we hoped to put it to good use. Our experts reported it was not high quality and worth next to nothing.

TRAVELING THROUGH PALESTINE

Three days later, I arrived in Baghdad on one of the riverboats. I brought Yusuf with me to Busra to help me board for the transition to Egypt. It was the first time Yusuf had been that far downstream. He compared what he saw with things related to his native town of Samarra. The cheap prices, variety of food in the bazaars at Busra were the only things that impressed him.

I ran into a few old friends. Through them I'd met Gen. Sutton, who rescued me from a dreary rest camp and allowed me into his home. The General asked me to go with him to Zobeir, where he was dedicating a hospital. Zobeir was a hot, desert town with around 10,000 residents, fifteen miles inland from Busra. The climate was cleaner and healthier. Many wealthier and prominent natives of the river towns had houses to stay in the hot summer months. To an outsider, this was an improvement from the suffocating hot air. The heat sprawled over all these coastal towns along the Persian Gulf. It was an uncomfortable and blistering heat.

Zobier's history was inherited from the tribesmen. Full

of caravans from Central Arabia. Many Turks felt the inhabitants were exempt from military service. A clear admission on the Turk's part. They didn't dare conscript the locals and force them to fight.. That gave the British a great triumph and a boost of confidence in the desert. A hospital opened for anyone that wanted to introduce innovative ideas among the desert communities.

The Sheikh of Zobier contributed much time and energy funding the transfer of land. Dr. Borrie, the man who ran the civil hospital, included Zobier in his medical check rounds. The Sheikh showed us the hospital. A cool, comfortable, and immaculate building. The Indian appointed as the resident physician had every sign of intelligence and skill.

The Sheikh gave us a sizeable Orthodox-style feast. A sheep was roasted whole, other meat-based dishes, and a variety of vegetables sprawled out on the table. While we ate, several men gave speeches. Gen. Sutton made a memorable address, translated to Arabic by an interpreter. Our Arabian hosts talked a good amount, the local orator was so classical in how he spoke, all the forms and tenses were impossible to translate. But I understood the gist of what he said. I brought a book called *Lusiads*, which I read when the speeches became more drawn-out than needed—these folks were long-winded.

I secured a seat on a British Indian boat named *The Torrilla*. It took passengers from the 3rd Division field artillery down to Egypt. As we made our way downstream, I watched an inconsolable Yusuf standing on the dock. Another chapter of my life had closed, and a fascinating one at that. I didn't have time to mull over what my next lot in life would be.

My reverie was broken from a cry of fire, next to where I

stood. In the smoking area through the open hatchways, soldiers rushed out and hurried to the lower decks. Since the ship carried quite a bit of ammunition, anything that happened would do so quickly. Only those in the right spots could help control the current events, I decided to stay exactly where I was. A few minutes passed and they put the fire out.

The 14-day trip through the Persian Gulf to the Red Sea was peaceful. I had no orders to follow and no duties to fulfill. I spent my time in the stables, wandering around in the lines of horses. The heat on the lower ship decks had less effect on the horses than I'd imagined. They were well cared for. Many horses were seasoned veterans that had been on a voyage before. If the information I was told was accurate, they had only lost one horse on the entire trip.

Most of the time, I spent laid back in my chair, reading whatever I could find around the ship and in the library. The radio went down a few days after we took off. We weren't able to communicate at all with the outside world. I gave up speculating what France would be like when we got there.

On the morning of June 4th, we dropped anchor in the Suez Harbor. We hoped that *The Torrilla* would make it all the way through the Port Said canal. But the disembarkation officer informed us we had to unload at the Suez and continue by train. I did so and traveled to Alexandria. I learned a convoy had just taken off by boat and wouldn't arrive for another two weeks. Sir Reginald Wingate was the British High Commissioner and a family friend. He and his wife extended the utmost hospitality. They insisted I move out to their residence and wait for the next boat.

Sir Reginald suggested I take advantage of the delay by going straight through Palestine. The trains had been running to Jerusalem, I could go from Cairo with only one change on the way. At Kantara is where I'd cross the canal, entering the military zone. I left at 11:30 a.m. and boarded the train to Ludd, where general headquarters was located. I arrived there by seven the next morning.

Everyone I'd met who knew Gen. Allenby was enthusiastic about him. After a few minutes in his company, I noticed their enthusiasm was justified. The General represented the model of a perfect British soldier. The morning I arrived, an attack was in progress, I heard the guns booming. The commander allowed me to use a car at my disposal. I visited some old friends I'd made in England and Mesopotamia before the war. Among my English friends was Col. Ronald Storrs, the military governor of Jerusalem, whom I'd spent many days with.

Life in The Holy City barely seemed affected by the war. There was an innovation at the Church of Nativity at Bethlehem. The different Christian-based religious sects, Greek and Latin Catholics, made the church a target. More than one death had resulted. It had been custom to have a recurring relief of Turkish soldiers stationed at the church. Their place now taken by the British, French, and Italians.

Each nationality had a rotation to furnish the guard for a day at a time. The Jerusalem population was mixed, most of them Christians. Many groups went out to the Holy Land together. An empty seat was common at their tables with the expectation that Christ would one day appear and occupy that seat. The Russians had their felt hats and frock coats that they wore everywhere. In the street, Jews would meet in the departing glory of Jerusalem by bowing their heads. They wore ancient derby hats.

A street in Jerusalem

One of the few strong buildings in Jerusalem was the Mosque of Omar, nicknamed the "Dome Of Rock," built on the legendary site of Solomon. The mosaics that lined the inside were stunning.

The simplicity is what captured me the most. Likely because the Christian holy places were gaudy, decorated with tin foil flowers and knock-off carvings. A hope was that Christians would someday unite and clear out all the terrible knick-knacks and clutter taken as offerings in the Church of the Holy Sepulchre.

Muslims held the Mosque of Omar second to the Great Mosque in the city of Mecca. The followers of Mohammed entered barefoot. They placed large yellow slippers as a requirement for all members. If they wore shoes, they had to wear the slippers over them.

It was no longer necessary to remove their hats, since it was not a sign of disrespect to Muslims, as they always kept on their red fez hats. The mosque was built by the Caliph Abd el Melek, 50 years after Omar captured Jerusalem in 636 AD. Many of the bricks and stones used in the building came from the temple of Jupiter. A famous giant rock in the center of town measured 60 feet wide and over six feet tall. To the Mohammedans, it was more sacred than anything else in the world, next to the Black Stone in Mecca.

Supposedly, it was at the rock where Abraham and Melchizedek sacrificed themselves to Jehovah. And where Abraham had brought Isaac as another offering. Scientists believed the temple altar had a channel to carry away the crimson blood of the victims. The Crusaders believed the Mosque was an original temple of Solomon.

According to their reports, they'd rededicated it to the massacre of over 10,000 Muslims that fled there to find refuge. The iron screen installed around the rock still stood. The cave below was still a traditional place of worship as used by several characters from the Old Testament, like David and Elijah. From it, Mohammed had made a night journey to heaven, riding his steed named El Burak. In the floor of the cave, an opening was covered by a simple slab of stone. It had instructions to head to the center of the world to be a communication device for the souls of the dead.

The military governor worked to improve the sanitary conditions in Jerusalem. The only water used by the natives had been rainwater gathered in tanks. Years earlier, it was suggested water be brought to the city via pipes. Some were already installed before the residents decided it was unrealistic. The British established a pipeline as well. It ran through the same reservoir that Pontius Pilate used to bring rainwater in through an aqueduct. They also built roads that wound through the hills. In Mesopotamia, I was struck by the conditions of buildings and how improvements were always being made. Even to the self-righteous people absorbed in their own rivalries. They were sure to gain freedom from Turkish rule.

The current situation in Palestine differed in many ways from Mesopotamia. Specifically, due to the benefit of being close to Egypt. On occasion, leaves were granted to go to Cairo or Alexandria. They allowed for a break with a complete change of environment. I'd never seen a capital so chipper and colorful. The Shepherd's Hotel was open and crowded, they danced as pleasant as ever.

The beaches off the coast of Ramleh were vibrant. Groups of sun-bathers gathered not far from Alexandria. The higher-ranking men proved their value by keeping the Army in line. Sections of the beach were reserved for non-commissioned officers and their comrades. While they were in Cairo, they took advantage of Pyramid sight-seeing tours and what guides described as "other points of interest."

When I left Mesopotamia, I decided to seek out a man in Palestine. I wanted to see if he was held over like I was. He was Major A.B. Paterson, known to Australians as "Banjo" Paterson. His two best-selling books were *The Man From Snowy River* and *Rio Grande's Last Race*. These books were popular and used as a source of daily quotes and inspiration. I hoped to one day meet this amazing author.

I knew he'd fought in the South African war, and that he joined with the Australian forces in Palestine. When I landed, I asked every Australian-appearing officer I ran into where to find Major Paterson. Locating a single member of an expeditionary force is never easy, no matter how well-known they are. Everyone knew him, but not where he was. When I told a man at Australian Headquarters I was searching for him, he turned to his comrade, "Say, where is Banjo now? At Moascar, right?"

Whether they'd ever met him in person was beyond me.

On my trip back to Alexandria, I stopped at Moascar, the center of the Australian Remount Service. This is where I found the author I'd searched so long for. A man in his 60s with a long mustache and powerful features. Much like the American Frederic Remington portrayed so well. He'd lived through everything he'd written.

At random periods throughout his life, he'd dove for pearls around the islands, herded sheep, bucked broncos. As well as anything in the wild of Australian life. The Australian natives told me he was to the best horse rider in Australia at his prime. He drove a herd 300 miles through Cairo and didn't lose a single animal. He proved to those who said a journey like that was not possible. Although he spent much of his time in England, Maj. Paterson had never been to the States. He had said that among the American writers he cared the most for, were the works of Joel Chandler Harris, and O. Henry. *What an odd combination.*

In Egypt, I met Col. Lawrence. He commanded the respect and admiration of everyone around him. Before the war, he engaged in archeological research under the direction of Professor Hogarth at Oxford University. Their most highly-regarded work was connected with the excavation of a buried city said to be underneath Palestine. At the outbreak of it all, Prof. Hogarth joined Naval Intelligence. He was considered priceless to the Egyptian Expeditionary Forces. Lawrence had a background in Arabic. He organized the desert tribes into groups that raided Turkish outposts and destroyed many of their communication lines.

He established a bodyguard of reckless outlaws. Men that, in old Western times, would be known as "bad men." They were devoted to him, and he counted on them remaining faithful if he ran into any obstacles. He dressed as an Arab but didn't make an effort to hide his true nationality. He'd send out a tribe to scatter and break the railways, blow up any bridges, and take any Turkish supplies beneficial to us. They swooped down like hawks in an open desert. They struck before the Turks could retaliate. Lawrence explained that he must succeed because if he failed to capture supplies, his reputation among the locals would end. Then, no one would trust or follow him anymore.

He found it difficult to kill his wounded. But the horror of falling into Turkish hands was a reality. He'd order the merciful killing of anyone badly injured or not able to be carried away by camel. The Turks offered a reward for Col. Lawrence and his men. A stunning 10,000 pounds if they were delivered as a dead body, or 20,000 pounds if they were wounded, but still alive. The living were more valuable because the Turks enjoyed a public execution.

Lawrence was eager to bring along an Englishman that would help figure out the best methods to blow up bridges and buildings. But he never found anyone able to take that long of a journey on a camel.

Barely over 30, a clean-shaven youthful face and a short, slender build. If I'd met him within a group of officers, it would've been challenging to single him out as someone with such power over the Arabs. Lawrence admired the Arabs and appreciated their many personalities. He looked up to their intelligence and sensitivity.

Once, when he was on the outskirts of Damascus, at that time, miles behind the Turk's battle lines. Lawrence and his men stopped at an empty palace in the desert. The Arabs took him on a tour through all the rooms, explaining that each one had a different aroma from perfumes they used inside. Although Lawrence maintained he couldn't smell any difference, his men claimed one had roses, one with jasmine, and another of ambergris. At the end of the tour, they came to a large and ruinous room. They told him, "This has the finest scent of all," and described the smells of the wind and sun.

The last I saw of Col. Lawrence was in Paris, he helped transport the future Kedjaz Prince to attend the Peace Conference.

When I returned to Alexandria, I discovered the convoy ships were still delayed until further notice. Three vessels suffered severe damage. One sunk and killed several passengers, another was damaged in the harbor by submarines lying in wait for any passing boats. I never discovered what the third was. The time and dates of departure were secret. They did not want to give any advance notice to enemies lurking nearby. Many troops embarked and waited in the harbor for days.

Transportation was filled to capacity, units were hurried off to halt the German advance in France. Casual officers were assigned to destroyers and cruisers in the direction of their travel to help. I was assigned to a tiny Japanese destroyer, called the *Umi*. She was roughly 650 tons when empty. The class of the boat within the Japanese Navy is smaller than ours. Umi was as clean as a pin, and the crew was too.

The officers were friendly and did everything possible to accommodate. They made everyone as comfortable as they could in the confined quarters. The first meal served on board, we used silverware. The Japanese preferred their chop-sticks. I loved to watch their skill using chopsticks, even under the most challenging circumstances. One morning when the boat bobbed in the wind more than usual, I arrived at breakfast to find a steward had brought in yolky eggs. I looked forward to watching someone eat that with chopsticks.

They all ate the eggs with such speed and ease and were off to complete their duties before I was done eating.

Japanese destroyers passing through Taranto

We departed Alexandria with an airplane escort. An observation balloon also stayed with us for a good part of our journey. The hazards and precautions were real. Two submarines were sighted shortly after we departed the harbor. The Japanese tradition was to execute everything with speed, we prepared for action. Every member was at their battle station. All guns readied for action in what seemed like record-time after the first warning signal. When we got closer to the Italian shore, I saw these giant destroyers at work.

A submarine shot, a fast torpedo passed the bow of another ship, barely missing it. It happened in a swoosh of water. The Japanese were right behind it. They swerved in and out of each other like a cat chasing a mouse and letting it rip until no longer visible. We maneuvered through the sea for another hour. We threw overboard any debris that shook our craft from the explosion, pools of water came aboard.

When we steamed into the familiar harbor of Taranto, it was a welcome sight. We charged through the narrow entrance. Passing refueling destroyers eagerly awaiting the chance to continue the fight.

AMERICAN ARMY IN FRANCE

U pon my transfer to the American Army, I was made a field artillery captain. I'd hoped to lead infantry. Just who made this wrong decision was beyond me. Once I got into the artillery field, I found it made the most sense to lay back. I felt obligated to take a course before going up to the line.

I left right away to the artillery school in Saumur. The leaders were half French and half American. Colonel McDonald and Col. Cross were the Americans in charge. The school had a terrific reputation due to their efficiency. Headquarters intended to gradually replace all the French leaders with American ones. During my time, the French were still dominant. We needed to wait until our leading officers learned how to use the French guns from personal experience.

When men learn new combat conditions, they must be ready to absorb everything taught. They must understand that under enemy fire, the situations will be filled with anxiety and nerves. This school was for officers and outside candidates. The non-officers were chosen from the troops of non-commissioned officers serving on the front line. After I learned this, I sent men from my battery to the first part of the course.

A difficult course for anyone without mathematical training, or if out of practice. Several excellent sergeants and colonels didn't have the necessary grounding to pass the exams. They should never have been sent there. It put them in an awkward, embarrassing position. No hard feelings were held if they failed. No one thought less of them.

The French officer in charge was Major DeCaraman. His dedicated service on the front lines, combined with his work ethic and initiative, made him an invaluable member to the team. He was a genius at working out ideas and coming up with methods for France and America. His house always seemed filled with Americans. This showed how much his hospitality meant to the soldiers across the ocean. The homes in France were open to us with welcoming arms.

The sincerity and goodwill we received had bestowed a debt upon my heart I hope to pay back one day. It was a cherished action acknowledged by everyone in our troop.

The town of Saumur is a delightful old one, right in the heart of France. The Loire River ran through it. Along the banks were caves, some with prehistoric paintings. I drew my finger across a painting of a man among beasts as he struggled for supremacy in the Dark Ages.

An impressive castle built on top of a hill dominated the town. One of the churches hung among an array of tapestries of various colors and designs. The well-kept roads made it easy to stroll along the riverbanks. Fishermen of all ages, sexes, and races sat alongside each other. Unshaken by the fact they never seemed to catch any fish. An older lady with a sunbonnet sat on a three-legged stool. She sat at the same spot almost every day, right up against the rocks. She had the same rusty, black umbrella to use if the sun became too strong.

The buildings used for our artillery course were also used by their cavalry school, known to be one of the best in the world. Before the war, Army officers from the Orient were ordered by their governments to follow these courses and learn the methods they taught. My old friend Fitzhugh Lee was one of those men sent by the US.

At the end of my instruction, I was put in command of the C Battery troop of the 7th Field Artillery during the Argonne battle. One morning, I stood in the desolate, shell-covered town of Landres. I watched lines of "doughboys," come toward me up the road. A battered and beaten Dodge car led them as they got closer. In the back seat sat my older brother Ted. He was in a deep discussion with one of his officers.

Last I had heard, he was at a staff school in Landres recovering from an injury. He recuperated and was offered command of the 26th Regiment, his original one. He made his way back to duty even though he was only registered to be back for light duty. I flagged my brother down, gave him a hug. We started talking until another car came up and out jumped my brother-in-law, Col. Richard Derby, the 2nd Division surgeon. We were the last three members of the family still on active duty. And here we were at the exact same place and time.

My brother Harry, the aviator, died when the Germans shot him down. My other brother John wounded his leg and arm and was evacuated to the United States. I wasn't sure of his condition at this time.

On November 11th, we returned to our original sector after we briefly attacked Sedan. None of us had confidence in an agreement being signed. We believed the Germans would never accept our terms. They could at best last until spring or summer. After that we could pursue an unconditional surrender.

When the shooting stopped. The news came that the enemy surrendered. There wasn't much reaction. We were cautious, weary that anything could happen. For the last two weeks, we'd been tossed back and forth. Deprived of sleep and food, our hope diminished with our supply of horses and men. The only signs of enthusiasm I heard were occasional trucks and staff cars. They passed through after dark with headlights blaring.

Shouts of "Lights out!" assured us the torturous reign was over. The men built fires and gathered, they yelled, "Lights out!" as each new fire started. A joke that never stopped being funny.

We were ordered to march into Germany and take over one of the bridges. The order came in an unclear and vague way. Within a few days, we were back out of the desolate ruins and into the village of Bantheville. We had five days to spend there. During this time, we'd be outfitted again. Our horses were not in the best shape. They'd trekked through rain and mud and had run down even the toughest of steeds.

During the endless evening marches, I saw the same two horses lean against each other in complete and utter exhaustion. As if saying they can't make it on either of their own. We were warned to be ready for anything and get the supplies needed to prepare our batteries.

African-American troops were instructed to make repairs on the roads. Some of us decided to sing for the men —quartet-style. We went to where they built shelters from iron sheets and random pieces of wreckage they'd picked from town. By then we'd collected four singers. We headed back to the shack for the 4th Division, where they were headed.

Everyone gathered on a platform built close to a raging fire of pine tree wood. Impressive clogging and singing echoed through the night. The big bass-toned singer wore his steel helmet. It added to his character while setting off his sharp features. His eyes gleamed in the flames of the fire.

The evening of the second day brought orders for us to take off the following morning. We were happy to get rid of some lesser-needed materials. The two days of rest and real food helped our horse situation. Our instructions were to salvage any ammunition, no matter what we got rid of. We were able to spare one horse for riding, my mare. She wasn't good at pulling if a car needed to be unstuck from the mud.

We left behind the little horse I'd ridden on several reconnaissance missions. My horse amused me in that she always had the determination to stay undercover. She never wanted to cut across any fields. She preferred to stick to the woods and trail, with no intention of exposing herself. Despite her continuous caution, it was because of her many wounds why she was the one we abandoned. I trusted she was going to reap the rewards of her hard work.

We were a sad-looking bunch as we marched from Bantheville. My lieutenants had lost their bedrolls and extra clothing. They traveled light and were told that anything we left behind would be taken care of. It would be there when we were moved to another sector. Nearly everything disappeared by the time they tried to gather our things. Although the horses were in poor shape, the men were fit for duty and ready to take on anything that was going to arise.

Our next destination was Malancourt, not far away. The roads were jam-packed, it was after nightfall before we reached the bleak hill reserved for us. It was frigid, and we gathered twigs and dead branches to make a fire. We found shell craters to sleep in. The ground was speckled with them. This couldn't have been done without extreme artillery.

France was an active area when it came to the war. Most of the towns were beaten and battered by the Germans, and then the French. We took a large part in further destruction of the ruins. The villages were recognizable from the left-over waste, and the signboards stuck in a random mound.

The following day we marched through Montzeville, Bethainville, landing at the Verdun-Paris Highway. Nine or ten tanks, varying from a small Renault up to a large, powerful battleship were strewn across the road. Some of the hits were stopped by the battleship. Others were far away from the targets, hitting hanging wires. A constant sight of ruined towns and desolate countrysides. It was a relief to walk through occasional villages where houses still stood, the beginning of the new world.

At 10 p.m., I'd gotten everyone from our battery into Balaicourt. Strong winds blew, the cold was intense. I sent off on foot to find tarps for the men so they could have a little bit of shelter. The town was deserted, except for the few remaining residents. I was able to provide everyone with some fashion of cover. Getting into these tents was a blessing in windy and rainy weather. The men were appreciative of being held over in peace that day. Even though there wouldn't be enough time to clean, bathe, or do laundry.

The next day we marched. Our first official advance into Germany. We located the Verdun Highway, which played an essential role in our defense. It broke the back of the German, a pleasant change from the shell-covered roads that we were so used to. I rode to the head of my battery, and onto the southern gate of Verdun. I followed the winding streets of the ancient city through to the other side. The road I was on had crossed a part of the famous Hindenburg line. Intact, evacuated by the Germans a few days prior under the terms of the armistice.

We halted where an African engineer regiment worked on making the road passable. An officer walked up to me and asked if I wanted any food. A foolish question when you're in the Army. A strong African cook brought me soup, roast beef, and coffee. I'd never appreciated the culinary arts of the French as much as I did for that meal. The food was a wonderful presentation of a rolling kitchen.

The cook looked like he'd have been able to introduce us to his French confidant Major DeCaraman told me about. The Frenchman was on his way out to an outpost with a hot pot of soup. He ran into a German who demanded he surrender. The cook reacted by slamming the soup dish over his head and marched him back to us as a prisoner. His capture had been rewarded with a medal, the *Croix de Guerre*.

It was interesting to see the German's method of defense still in one piece. Not yet shattered by our artillery. The wires went on for miles, riding alongside the mined trees and roadsides. This was done by cutting a groove of about three inches in length and depth and filling it with explosives. The purpose was to block off the road in case we had to retreat. Only a few of the mines seemed to have been set off.

We passed through several towns that appeared to no longer exist. When we arrived in Etain, many buildings still stood strong, although gutted. The cellars were converted into dugouts with different passages added. We sheltered in small German huts on the outskirts. They were well dug out and comfortably fitted for one person. We prepared to camp there for a few days as instructed. But by midnight, orders changed to be ready to leave the next morning.

The country was lovely and gave little sign of German occupation. When we passed through villages, the signs were in German. There was little originality in the street names. You were sure to find a Hindenburg, Kronprinz, and at least one named after the Kaiser.

The mile posts were replaced, but they were battered metal plaques from the Automobile Touring Club of France. Ever since we'd left Verdun, we kept running into bands of recently-released prisoners. Mostly Italian or Russian with a few French and English. Sapped and underfed, their clothes looked like worn rags. A few had put their belongings onto little cars, like children would make out of soapboxes. The trucks returned back to base after bringing up the rations and took back as many men as they could carry.

We barely came across any civilians before we reached Bouligny. Once a bustling and prosperous town. Few residents were allowed to stay in their homes during the occupation. Small groups of removed residents cautiously returned, trickling back in. The invaders had destroyed their property, buildings were gutted. The German soldier's habits were always unexplainable to me. They preferred to live in filth. When we'd re-captured the châteaux, they'd been converted into complete pigsties.

The residents went wild once we arrived. The smaller villages left their homes carrying wreaths, throwing confetti and flowers. They shouted "*Marseillaise*," the French National Anthem. Infantry marched in advance to the center of the celebration. Bands made up of young children, no older than 5 years old, danced in the streets to the singing of the anthem. It must've been taught and practiced behind closed doors. The bands were often made up of an American soldier or two singing and dancing in full swing, absolutely enjoying themselves. The entertainment seemed natural, not inspired by alcohol. I knew this because the Germans took with them everything there was to drink.

Bouligny was not an attractive place, as few manufacturing towns were. We had gotten the men in shelter under some waterproof covers, and were able to heat up water to get some washing done. My striker found a large caldron so I could take a bath. *Luxurious*. The first I had in over a month. What made it even better was having clean clothes to put on once I was done.

One evening when we returned from a nearby village, I ran into a civilian wearing a large frock coat. He asked me in German how to get to Etain. I asked him who he was, he replied that he was German but sick of his country and willing to go anywhere else. He didn't appear to be a spy (and even if he was, I didn't have any use for him). I pointed him in a direction, and we never met again. I still wonder what became of that man.

The German Soldiers didn't expect to surrender their conquests. They built a huge fountain made of stone and brick right in the center of the town. Inscribed with a chisel was the name "*Hindenburg Brunnen*." Hanging above the German commissary shop was a wooden board that read "*Gott strafe England*." A slogan used in the war meaning "May God punish England." This showed the bitterness of the Huns toward Great Britain. There were no British troops within the sectors at the head of this section of invaded territory.

We worked hard to armor-up and get our equipment ready in the few days we stayed in Bouligny. One morning, several townspeople leaked into the village. They wore their best clothes, likely buried in their cellars or attics to greet the President and First Lady Poincaré. They'd come to visit the most important of their recently-liberated towns. It was so cheerful to hear the applauding. We watched all the locals plastered with smiling faces lighting up like the sun.

On November 21st, we continued on. Once we got closer to the border, we came upon a large, German cemetery artistically laid out. A massive group of statues stood in the middle of it. Life-sized granite statues of famous German soldiers in full gear stood out. As we walked on, I focused on the stones that marked the boundary lines between Lorraine and France. I was walking through history, as well as being a part of it.

We entered Aumetz and the elder townspeople greeted us with open arms in French. The town was filled with vibrant colors created from who knows where. Children tried to balance on top of the barrels of abandoned German cannons. They climbed all over the giant, camouflaged trucks. Not realizing how far we'd gone, we'd gotten to the border where France, Luxemburg, and Lorraine all met. We spent the day skirting the borders of one, then the other, and stopping for the night in the French town of Villerupt.

Everyone went wild when we rode in. We were apparently the first Allied soldiers any had seen. We were made to feel welcome. The townsfolk offered us German champagne (which tasted terrible). They threw a reception with whole-hearted speeches and the kindest words for our war effort.

I bunked up with the mayor, Monsieur Georges. After dinner, he pulled out two dusty bottles of Brut champagne. He changed their hiding place at least four times and forgot the last place was in the cellar.

It seemed they were made for that night of absolute

liberation. Msr. Georges was thin and haggard. He'd spent two years in the solitary confinement sector of the prison for having given a French prisoner some bread to eat. His 18-year-old daughter was put in prison for a year due to not informing authorities about what her father did—assuming she knew about it.

Not a single family learned any of the German language. This was because all French civilians were required to salute the Germans every Sunday. They lined up in the market-place for the general muster. The details of how they came to forgive their oppressors were foggy and complicated.

The men behind the lines knew the consequences of the sullen events. But the soldiers on the front lines believed Germany won and was setting their terms. To honor them-selves, they came through with wreaths hung atop their bayonets while singing victory songs.

I wondered how they distributed the food supply America sent to the inhabitants of the invaded districts. I asked Monsieur Georges, who had assured me that they were careful. They feared if they didn't use caution, the supplies may no longer be sent and would have to dip into their own scarce resources. The mayor explained the joy when the shipments were received and how the people called their ration-pickings "Going to America."

We sat and talked for hours into the night before going to bed. I retired to a luxurious bed with the cleanest linen sheets I'd seen in ages. No trouble finding shelter for our men. The townsfolk seemed to fight over who stayed with whom.

I woke the next morning, disappointed at how soon we had to leave our amazing hosts. But we marched off into the small Duchy of Luxemburg. We passed through a thriving city called Esch, famous for its iron mines. The streets were filled with colorful flags, as many Italian flags as there were French, since Esch supported a large Italian colony. Brass bands paraded in our honor, who we later met in many of the smaller villages we passed by. The shops were full, and prices steep. The Germans abandoned the Luxemburg people to fend for themselves. They looked pleased to see us since it likely meant the end of the isolation they'd grown accustomed to, and their soldiers would return home.

We rode along the lovely countryside. Filled with smiling fields and hills made it seem remote, yet peaceful. It felt unnatural to pass through a village with empty, intact houses, and not having to use them for shelter. This was such a change compared to the battered and shell-covered France.

We were in the wake of the German Army. They retired in an orderly manner and left little behind. Our first night, we camped at the village of Syren, five miles from the capital. Finding shelter was harder here since we were instructed to treat everyone as equals. No one liked the thought of having soldiers stay with them. It seemed the people of Luxemburg were friendly to us because that was their policy. The chalk marks the officers put on the doors had not washed off. We were able to tell how many men could be lodged at one time in that particular house.

Where I lodged, seemed to have the friendliest host, as mine was French. Her nephew came from Paris to visit a few months before the war started and wasn't able to get back into France. To avoid the dread of temporary camps, he passed as a civilian of Luxemburg. In the regiment, many men had parents that came from Duchy. They spoke German and had acquired a popularity within their groups of comrades. They made friends with some villagers and arranged to hand over their rations for the housewives to cook.

The diplomat usually invited a few friends to enjoy the much-needed change from the sloppy food served out of caldrons from the battery's rolling kitchen. I assumed many men in my battery were able to speak German, mostly by looking at their last names. When it came time to prove it, I found that I had four men total that spoke fluent enough to use as interpreters.

The next morning, we made a winding march to Trintange, since there was no direct way to get there. Here we stood, instructed to be ready to settle down for a week or more, we could've ended up in a much worse spot. The country was broken up by hills and ravines. Small patches of forests and streams bounced down the rocky channels. It reminded me of Rock Creek Park in Washington. The weather was perfect. Nippy air in the morning, then out came the sun from behind the hills.

The officer in charge of shelter assignments did well on our final part of the march into Coblenz. I now had all my officers. Lieutenants Furness, Middleditch, Pearce, and Brown. During battle, they were stricter in some ways but too relaxed in others.

In the American Army, less responsibility was given to officers and corporals then in England. More so in the spirit and efficiency of the entire organization that depended on its lower-ranking officers.

We were fortunate to have a level-headed bunch, including Sgt. Cushing, who was a veteran of the Spanish War. He'd been a sailor for several years, and after leaving the sea became a warden in his home state of Massachusetts. In the peak of it, he was the only strength relied on among his troop and set the example.

The first sergeant was an old Army man, knowledgeable in drills and routines that were of extreme value. He understood the profession and everything that came along with it. He assisted in training our young men and was relied upon under tough conditions.

One afternoon I strolled into Luxemburg with Col. Collins, a battalion commander. The town looked medieval from afar. It may have been over a castle wall that Kingsley's knight spurred on his horse for his final leap. The village of Altenahr was not far away, where poets would find their muse. The town was structured along the cliffs that outlined a deep, rocky canyon only passable by a few old stone bridges. The massive entry gates opened at the passes tunneled through the hills. Broad streets and town squares with narrow passageways wound around the ancient quarters.

I entered a large bookstore to replenish my mobile library. I was awed by the large quantity of postcards that had the Marshal, King, and Queen of Belgium on them. I noted they were printed in Leipzig, I asked the worker how that was possible. He told me he got them from a traveling German salesman. He added he was shocked at the samples he'd been given.

The salesman assured him that the postcards would be easy to sell in Luxemburg, and if that was really the case, he was okay with displaying them. A one-off card of King Albert stood tall with a drawn sword and a caption:

"You shall not violate the sacred soil of my country."

One publication that piqued my interest in a weekly paper was written in English, even though it was produced in Hamburg, Germany. It was full of jokes and notes from

Germans that explained difficult words or phrases improperly translated. Even with their hatred of England, the Germans continued to try to learn English.

Thanksgiving Day came, and we set out to provide a special feast. The best we could put together. It proved to be tricky. No exchanges were able to be made or regulated, so lower rates were not valid at the time. Someone had come from Paris with enough money to help us get a suckling pig. Mess Sergeant Braun roasted it inside of the priest's oven. He even put in the traditional apple in the pig's mouth—I still don't know the purpose for—but the stuffing that came out was terrific. We washed it down with fantastic white wine from Moselle. We were only a few miles away from the vineyards that ran along the riverbank.

That afternoon, I borrowed a bicycle from the mayor and rode to the village of Elmen. I ran into my brother again. He'd just sat down for his own Thanksgiving feast served by two Asian men from his regiment. After talking with him and helping myself to some more food, I made my way back, but not before getting drenched in the rain.

The next day, we paid our men, the first time in nearly a year for some of them. To withdraw their pay, payroll had to be signed at the end of each month and be on-hand at the end of the following month to pay them out. No one was able to sign unless the service records were at hand, sent to the hospital by relaying it through the military if a man was sick or injured. The documents wouldn't make it back to his assigned unit until many months after he would have returned.

This caused a hardship for the men. The military tried to regulate the amount they'd give so the men wouldn't spend it on alcohol or gambling. We had always tried to make someone that had the highest debt either pay a deposit or send money back home. The YMCA Secretary was Mr. Harlow, he was attached to our regiment. He helped out a great deal when it came to getting the money transferred to the States. The men would gamble before the money was even there, promising to pay when it arrived in a few days. They risked appallingly high amounts when they had no actual money on them. On this particular payday, we knew the wine and beer supply within the village wasn't high, so they couldn't cause too much trouble.

Orders were given to not purchase any cognac or hard liquor. Of course, a handful still managed to obtain some, always looking over their shoulders.

GERMANY AND HOME AGAIN

On December 1st, we resumed our march. We passed through Wormeldange and crossed the Moselle River into Hunland. Civilians lined the streets in both villages. Most of them just out of uniform, scowling as we rode past, muttering nonsense under their breath. We found a quick way out and ran into men still in field uniforms. They smiled at us but didn't pay our men any attention.

We then hit Onsdorf, our intended destination, and the officer in charge reported that he'd arrived with minimal difficulty.

The residents were anxious to please in any way possible. They weren't of Prussian descent and were sick and tired of the war. Still, it seemed their attitude was negative towards us, lacking any dignity whatsoever. I couldn't tell if it was of their own initiative, or if they were instructed how to act. Probably a combination, we heard warnings that Germans were planning to poison American officers. We never saw any actual proof.

The next morning we crossed the Saar River and followed it down to where it connected with the Moselle

River. The woods and ravines were beautiful but proved challenging to travel through on our horses. We marched through the oldest town in Germany, Treves, with a population of about 30,000 residents.

During the 4th Century, a Roman poet born in France referred to it as "Rome beyond the Alps" due to the array of Roman remains. We stopped for some time in Porta Nigra. It had a huge fortified gateway that dated back to the first century, with additions made during the thirteenth. One of the most famous treasures was the Holy Coat of Treves, believed to be the most perfect garment created and worn by Christ at his crucifixion. The most prominent religion in this area was Roman Catholic. Pilgrims often exhibited his coat in the town.

We left Treves the next day and continued down the riverbanks to Rawen Kaulin where we decided to turn a few miles toward the inlands. I was assigned to the village of Eitelsbach, the residents looked terrified as we rode in. Several men ran and hid while the women cried in terror in front of their homes. I assumed they expected to be treated like the French treated the Belgians. When they realized we weren't going to harm them, they became willing to admire and serve. I had my first meal inside of the schoolmaster's home. He'd been a non-commissioned officer of the infantry. We talked about the war, and he harbored no ill will. His daughters played piano for us after we ate.

The country we marched through for the next few days was gorgeous. We followed a winding trail along the river that made "S" turns. The steep hills ran right into the riverbanks, and often a road would be cut short. A tiny village tucked into a flat plain between a hill and river. When the sun hit the slopes, it gave a sunny southern exposure. I saw many grapevines, planted with precision. Every nook and cranny in the rocks were filled. Farming this land had to have been difficult since soil was covered by pieces of mud.

The person working on this masterpiece had to have gained some impressive lung capacity to scale those rocky hillsides. The leaves had fallen, the naked vines covered in various colors showing occasional patches of evergreens.

Once or twice, the road separated from the river and cut across the mountains. This cost our horses a good amount of energy having to drag wood up the steep and slippery trail. What was the difference between those that lived along the riverbank and those who lived in the higher plateaus? The latter appeared more unusual and less prosperous. The highlands were covered in a mist. From farther away I made out the dim outlines of horses and men as if I were leading a ghost battery through the fog.

We were in the middle of wine country. Anyone that enjoyed a good bottle of champagne, the names of Berncastel and Piesport were familiar. In the last town, I was amused passing by a woman's hat store with the name, Jacob Astor. The smaller villages were victims of fairy tales created by Hans Anderson and The Grimm Brothers. The houses had wooden balconies connected in every place. They overlooked the winding roads that plastered over the cobblestones. Perched upon column beams were proudly-displayed gargoyles, dwarfs, and demons. Along with other strange creatures I couldn't make out. Houses had plaques on them to display when they'd been built, with the initials of the first person or couple to buy and live there.

I didn't see any dates before the late 1600s, although many of these houses were built before then. The doors, in some cases, were carved and withered. Old pumps and wells, stone bridges, and wayside shrines took this area back centuries. The records carved on the walls of the houses showed flooding was frequent. The highest flood mark I noticed was in 1685, and the last one was marked in 1892.

The population was well-fed, old and young. There were rumors of food shortages, and the Germans stressed over their food supply while surrendering. As far as I could tell, food was not in short supply. It seemed they had more food here than in France. Leather and rubber were scarce, many women wore pairs of army boots. Shoes displayed in shop windows were made from some type of pasteboard material. The coffee was ground from the berry of a special kind of native bush, the taste was nothing like coffee I'd drank before. The beer had fallen from its pre-war glory. Even still, the essentials of life appeared to be working for the inhabitants far more than we were led to believe.

We didn't run into too much trouble. A few sporadic instances where people stood in our way and vocally opposed our quartering of troops. We paid little attention other than making sure they followed our orders. We had amusing chats about war news with our soldiers. A man in my troop housed among several of my sergeants asked how much damage the Zeppelins caused to New York. And whether Philadelphia was evacuated because of the Germans.

Our men behaved well during this journey. There were occasional spouts of drunkenness. A few men took advantage of a country where wine was offered at a cheap cost. Few minor offenses and AWOLs. I reformed the last few men that were consistently late.

When we weren't in the camps, it was harder to keep people in order. They wandered through town, living a more comfortable life than their comrades. It took a lot of integrity to make this situation better. Whenever I had an opportunity, I stopped it from going any further. This lifted the spirit of our group as a unit.

We had an exceptional group of men, no matter where they hailed from. One of the buglers in my group had been born in Germany and brought up in Austria. The attendance list of the battery read like a League of Nations. Still, we were all loyal to the United States.

* * *

TWELVE DAYS after crossing the river from Luxemburg, we marched into Coblenz. We quartered in large barracks made of brick that sat on the city's outskirts, which the Germans left in terrible shape. Hercules himself would have felt cleaning the Augean stables was an easy task by comparison. We set out to work immediately and had all men and horses well-sheltered. The energy in the town was vibrant, the stores were well-stocked, and trade still thrived. I went inside a café where a great orchestra was playing and had some mediocre "war beer."

I headed off to the Turkish bathhouse. The one I found had a manager that was an ex-submarine sailor. In the steam room, I wondered if he was going to try and pull any tricks since I was the only one there. The last time I had one was in a wine-vat a week before. I was ready to risk anything at that point for a good soak.

Our orders to march the next day came at midnight. An orderly from our regiment's headquarters woke us in the middle of the night with marching instructions. Half-asleep, I was in no frame of mind to absorb this.

We made our way, the rain poured down, the mist dripped over the town and across the Pfaffendorf Bridge showing the dim outlines of Ehrenbreitstein. This fortress towered in front of us. The men were tired and cold. I heard a few comments about the size, as they expected it to be a Bridge that was the width of the Mississippi River. We found that the wet and slippery stones from the street to the river were challenging to navigate. It was a safe way to come up, and we pushed on at a steady pace. We struck off toward the bridge, our orders were to occupy the bridge for an undetermined length of time.

The Germans had torn down the signs that labeled the roads. As if the roads weren't complicated enough to begin with. Our horrible map didn't help either. I speculated taking down the signs was to confuse us—a success.

Great stone slabs piqued our interest, they were mounted around the 18th Century and showed distance in hours. I remember one of them claimed that it took three hours to get to Coblenz from where we were, and 18 to Frankfort. Never before or after that did I see these types of records.

Our march wasn't eventful. We thought getting to Coblenz was our goal. The idea was altered based on the downpour during our march through the valley of Moselle. This made for a long uncomfortable journey through the mud in our soaked clothes.

We reached the village of Niederelbert. Lt. Brown was the sheltering officer and had our assignments ready. It wasn't long before we got out of our soaked clothes.

My officers and I belonged to the Reserve Corps. None of us looked forward to a long garrison tour on the Rhine, or anywhere else for that matter. Lt. Brown distinguished himself with liaison work within the infantry, and held a temporary commission within the Army. He was eager to get back to civilian life as soon as possible. In Germany, the prospects were gloomy, there'd be no commingling with the natives like we did in France to lighten the dreadful moments.

Days later, our regiment headquarters coveted the village, and we were moved a few miles down the hills to Holler. We set off to make ourselves as comfortable as possible. I had a small Finnish fellow named Jahoola, an amazing man in every way. He took great care of my horse and maintained my shelter if it needed repairs. He seemed to do more with less and never stopped impressing.

The men continued to behave, and the German civilians didn't give us much trouble. When we settled into our shelters, we had the villagers clean up the streets and all the yards until the town looked good enough to be proud of. We policed any messes caused and kept the residents liable. The head of the household where I stayed told me his son was a captain in the Army, but deserted before the armistice. He arrived home in civilian clothes three weeks after the army retreated. He was never a war officer or enrolled in a military school. Still, the fact that his family was proud of him spoke a thousand words, showing discipline and morale.

After getting settled and making our own routines, I was glad to have my books with me. Of these, O. Henry had been my favorite, and most popular. I had read so many of the different editions that they were falling apart. I was surprised by how popular this book was among the English.

I brought with me other Oxford books like *Monsereau* and *Monte Cristo*, in both French and English, and even a couple in Portuguese and Spanish. It was possible to get books through the mail, even though it could take months.

Soon after we reached the end of the bridge, regular army officers turned up from a variety of schools where they'd been sent to become instructors. We hoped to be released in a similar manner.

Garrison duties should have been taken on by civilians. This would also allow the tradesmen to return to their standard and necessary positions. We searched around to get familiar with the country and keep our units in the best shape possible. In case any inclement weather or enemy surprises came about. The horses also required special attention. We felt rewarded once we saw their health improve. Many times we were unable to properly isolate our horses and men. We had to be innovative to make it work.

The men spent much of their time getting ready for inspection. Boots and clothing that were in one piece were also on short supply. We had to get along the best we could with what we had. Now that we were stationary, nearly everything we wanted was able to be supplied. The most significant hardship was the lack of exercise and recreation. The reading room was opened and had a piano inside. But there was nowhere else to go for a short trip or to send men anywhere, and little to do with their days off. Trips down the Rhine were planned. I believe they proved beneficial in problem-solving when it came to relaxation and amusement.

My father sent money to my brother and me to help make a Christmas Day feast for our men. It was challenging to get much, but the YMCA helped me get chocolate, cigarettes, and a couple of calves from the local markets. While it wasn't the Arabian feast I hoped for, we had the essentials. The men had high spirits and were ready to make the best of it.

In mid-January, I joined my brother and we left for Paris. I was sad to leave the battery, we'd been through so much together. Now that all the fighting had ended, I wanted to get back to my wife and children. The train made the distance without a glitch, especially in comparison to a march. The familiar sights of the French villages off in the distance were *oh-so-welcome* to me.

After several tough months on duty in France and Germany, I took passage on a transit boat from Brest to New York. I said goodbye to Mesopotamia and Europe, for now.

EDITOR'S NOTE

While Captain Frank Wooten's involvement in WWI ended here. His fame as a war hero grew. He received a promotion to Major and was awarded a World War I Victory Medal for valor in the War. He found himself an instant celebrity after returning home to Long Island and reuniting with his wife and children.

Frank struggled to build a new life after the war. The constant demand on his time and energy became too much for him, and like many WWI veterans he turned to drink. In 1921 he booked passage from New York to Havana on board the SS *Toloa*. The first night out to sea he had dinner with the captain and left the smoking room just after midnight.

He stated he was retiring for the evening but was never seen again. I'll let you guess what happened, although there is no proof either way. His body was never recovered.

I hoped you enjoyed this story and reading this book. I encourage you to write a review here. Also, visit WarHistory-Journals.com to view our other stories.

ALSO BY WAR HISTORY JOURNALS

BROKEN WINGS: WWI FIGHTER ACE'S STORY OF ESCAPE AND
SURVIVAL

*"A masterfully told story of triumph and redemption in a powerfully
drawn survival epic."* – Reviewer

Hero WWI Fighter Pilot Shot Down and Captured.

With an engaging and authentic retelling of his experiences as an
escaped prisoner of war, this gripping account details the life and
struggles of a captured pilot in 1917 war-torn Europe.

Lieutenant John Ryan couldn't wait to see action in WWI. He
joined up with the British colors out of Canada. As one of several
American pilots in the Royal Flying Corps before the US joined
the war, he earned his wings and became an Ace through fierce air
battles over the skies of Germany.

WORLD AT WAR: UNFORGETTABLE TALES FROM THE FIRST AND
SECOND WORLD WARS

"True Stories of Endurance, Horror and Beautiful Human Beings." –
Reviewer

Haunting Truths We Must Never Forget.

Follow in the footsteps of the British, German and American
servicemen as they detail the life and struggles of war in
mysterious and foreign countries. Uncover their mesmerizing,
realistic stories of combat, courage, and distress in readable and
balanced stories told from the front lines.

This book brings you firsthand accounts of combat and
brotherhood, of captivity and redemption, and the aftermath of

wars that left no community unscathed in the world. These stories have everything from spies and snipers to submarines and air raids. A great book for anyone who wants to learn what it was like during the world war conflicts between 1914-1945.

MONGOOSE BRAVO: VIETNAM: A TIME OF REFLECTION OVER EVENTS SO LONG AGO

"A frank, real, memoir" – Reviewer

Uncover the gritty, real-life story of a Vietnam combat veteran.

With an engaging and authentic retelling of his experiences as an infantry soldier of the B Co., 1/5th 1st Cavalry Division in the Vietnam War, this gripping account details the life and struggles of war in a strange and foreign country.

Printed in Great Britain
by Amazon